"UNDERCOVER CHRONICLES INSIGHTS INTO INDIAN PRIVATE DETECTIVES"

TELL ALL TEXTBOOK FOR PRIVATE INVESTIGATORS IN INDIA

CHENNAMALLIKARJUN C BHUSANUR

Made with ♥ on the Notion Press Platform
www.notionpress.com

In loving memory of my father Late Shri Channabasappa Bhusanur

& to

To the silent guardians, the tireless trackers, the discreet discoverers – the unsung heroes of the investigation industry.

This book is dedicated to you. Your dedication, resourcefulness, and unwavering pursuit of truth often go unnoticed, yet your contributions are invaluable. You navigate the shadows, meticulously gather evidence, and paint a clear picture where there was once only obscurity.

You are the backbone of private investigations, the invisible threads that weave together a compelling narrative. You work tirelessly behind the scenes, ensuring the investigator's success and the client's peace of mind.

This book is a testament to your expertise and a token of appreciation for your unwavering commitment to the profession. May your skills continue to be honed, your intuition remain sharp, and your contributions continue to be recognized.

With deepest gratitude,

Chennamallikarjun Bhusanur

Contents

Contents

Contents

Contents

Contents

Preface

A Calling Unveiled: My Journey into the World of Indian Private Investigations

For over three and a half decades, I, Chennamallikarjun Bhusanur, have had the privilege of traversing the intricate and ever-evolving landscape of private investigations in India. At C.C. Bhusanur, Investigation & Research Pvt. Ltd, we are a team forged by experience, specializing in preventive measures, uncovering the truth behind insurance claims, and ensuring the integrity of corporate operations. Our network of seasoned investigators stretches across Karnataka, and together, we bring a wealth of knowledge and a relentless pursuit of truth to every case we undertake.

This book isn't simply born from theory; it's the culmination of countless investigations, late nights piecing together puzzles, and the satisfaction of delivering results. But the journey wasn't always straightforward. The world of private investigations in India is a dynamic one, constantly adapting to evolving legal frameworks and technological advancements. Ethical considerations are paramount, and navigating the legalities can feel like a labyrinth at times.

That's where this handbook comes in. Imagine it as a trusted companion, a guide I wish I had when I first started. Whether you're a seasoned investigator seeking to refine your skills or an aspiring one eager to embark on this path, these pages hold valuable knowledge. We'll delve into the ethical principles that form the bedrock of our profession, explore the legalities of initiating civil cases, and unpack the intricacies of the PDAR Bill and its potential impact. Practical considerations like evidence collection, mastering the art of surveillance, and crafting clear and concise reports will all be meticulously explored.

Remember, the pursuit of truth is a lifelong journey. This handbook equips you with the tools and knowledge to navigate the complexities of the profession, but the quest for continuous learning is essential. As the legal landscape and industry standards evolve, so too must your skillset. Embrace the challenge, hone your craft, and uphold the highest ethical standards – that's the recipe for a successful and rewarding career as a private investigator in India.

Here's to embarking on this adventure together!

Sincerely,

Chennamallikarjun Bhusanur

Acknowledgements

Acknowledgement

the journey of bringing this book to fruition has been enriching and wouldn't have been possible without the support of many. First and foremost, I want to express my gratitude to the ever-vevolving world of Artificial Intelligence (AI) platforms. their ability to process information and generate creative text formats proved invaluable in shaping the ideas and structure of this handbook.

i am also deeply indebted to my esteemed colleages and partners in the Private Investigation profession. The countless discussions , shared experiencees, and unwavering support have been instrumental in my professional growth and development of the concept explored in this book.

Furthermore, I extend my heartfelt thanks to my friends, whose unwavering encouragement fueled my passion and kept me motivated throughout this project. Their belief in my vision and their willingness to offer constructive feedback have been truly motivating.

Finally, and most importantly, I want to express my deepest gratitude to my wife, Nirmala Bhusanur, and my son Akhil Bhusanur. Their unwavering patience and understanding provided a constant source of strength during the time invested in crafting this book. Without their unwavering support, thos project would have remained just a collection of ideas.

Thank you all for playing a significant role in making this book a reality.

The Foundations of Private Investigation

- Chapter 1: A Look Back, A Leap Forward: The Pioneering Spirit and Enduring Legacy of Private Investigation (This chapter sets the historical context for the profession)
- Chapter 2: The Investigator's Edge: Mastering the Art of Private Investigation in India (This chapter provides a general overview of the core skills and knowledge required)
- Chapter 3: Unveiling the Truth: Ancient Investigation Techniques in India (This chapter explores historical investigative practices in India)
- Chapter 4: Investigating a Changing Landscape: Techniques in Medieval and Colonial India (This chapter delves into investigative methods during specific historical periods)
- Chapter 5: Unveiling the Truth in a Modern Nation: Investigations in Post-Independence India (This chapter examines the evolution of investigations in modern India)

CHAPTER ONE

A Look Back, A Leap Forward: The Pioneering Spirit and Enduring Legacy of Private Investigation

The world of private investigation boasts a rich and fascinating history. In this chapter, we delve into the life of a remarkable individual who is considered the father of modern criminology and, arguably, the world's first private detective - Eugène-François Vidocq. Additionally, we'll explore some intriguing facts and lesser-known aspects of this captivating profession.

Eugène-François Vidocq: From Criminal to Crime Fighter

Born in 1775, Vidocq's life was a whirlwind of adventure and intrigue. His early years were marked by a stint in the French army followed by a descent into a life of crime. However, a fateful arrest in 1809 presented him with a unique opportunity. He offered his expertise in criminal activity to the French authorities in exchange for leniency. This proposition led to the creation of the first known criminal investigation bureau, with Vidocq at its helm.

Vidocq's unconventional methods, which often involved employing former criminals as informants, proved surprisingly successful. He was credited with apprehending a significant number of criminals while simultaneously blurring the lines between law enforcement and the underworld.

Intriguing Facts and Hidden Gems of the Profession

The world of private investigation is brimming with fascinating stories and surprising realities. Here are a few titbits to pique your curiosity:

- **The Rise of the Female Investigator:** Though often overshadowed in history, women have played a crucial role in private investigation for centuries. From pioneering figures like Kate Warne, the first female private detective in the United States, to the growing number of female investigators today, women have brought a unique perspective and skillset to the profession.
- **The Evolution of Technology:** Technology has become an indispensable tool for private investigators. From advanced surveillance techniques to sophisticated data analysis, technology allows investigators to gather information and solve cases with greater efficiency and accuracy.
- **The Moral Compass:** Ethical conduct is the cornerstone of a successful and respected private investigator. Maintaining confidentiality, respecting individual rights, and adhering to legal boundaries are essential for

building trust with clients and upholding the integrity of the profession.

- **Beyond Crime Solving:** Private investigators are not just about catching criminals. They are often called upon to conduct background checks, investigate insurance fraud, and locate missing persons. The scope of their work is diverse and constantly evolving.

Learning from the Past, Shaping the Future

Understanding the history of private investigation, particularly the pioneering spirit of figures like Vidocq, provides valuable lessons for aspiring investigators. It highlights the importance of innovation, ethical conduct, and adapting to the ever-changing landscape of the profession. As you embark on your journey as a private investigator, remember that you are part of a long and storied tradition. Upholding the highest standards of professionalism and embracing new knowledge will enable you to contribute to the continued evolution of this dynamic field.

Further Exploration:

This chapter serves as a springboard for further exploration. Consider researching the lives of other historical figures who have shaped the field of private investigation. Additionally, explore resources that delve deeper into the ethical considerations and legal frameworks governing private investigators in India.

By understanding the past and embracing the future, you can ensure that your career as a private investigator is not only successful but also contributes to the continuing legacy of this fascinating profession.

CHAPTER TWO

The Investigator's Edge: Mastering the Art of Private Investigation

While there's no official licensing for private investigators in India, a good one follows a well-defined process to uncover the truth. Here's a breakdown:

1. **Intake and Consultation:** The investigator meets the client to understand the situation. This could involve missing person cases, pre-marital checks [example: verifying a potential spouse's background], embezzlement suspicions [example: a company suspecting an employee of stealing funds], or gathering evidence for a civil case.
2. **Planning and Strategy:** The investigator devises a plan based on the case. This might involve surveillance [example: following someone to see their activities], discreet interviews with people who know the subject, or digging into public records for information like

property ownership or past addresses.

3. **Information Gathering:** This is where the detective puts their skills to the test. They might conduct interviews with witnesses or acquaintances of the subject, keeping in mind legal boundaries. They can utilize public databases or resources to find relevant details.
4. **Surveillance and Observation:** Depending on the case, discreet surveillance might be necessary. This could involve tailing someone or monitoring their movements in public places.
5. **Documentation and Evidence Collection:** Throughout the investigation, the investigator meticulously documents everything – notes from interviews, photographs, and any other relevant findings.
6. **Analysis and Reporting:** Once all the pieces are gathered, the investigator analyzes the information to form a conclusion. They then present a comprehensive report to the client, outlining the findings and any evidence collected.

Important Note: It's crucial to remember that Indian law restricts certain methods. Private investigators cannot impersonate law enforcement, tap phones, or trespass on private property. Their role is to gather information ethically and legally.

CHAPTER THREE

Unveiling the Truth: Ancient Investigation Techniques

Long before modern forensics and surveillance equipment, ancient India boasted a sophisticated system of investigation. Here's a glimpse into some of these fascinating techniques:

1. Observational Skills: Honing their powers of observation was paramount for investigators. Early texts like the Arthashastra emphasized the importance of analyzing a person's body language, facial expressions, and behavior for clues. Imagine a skilled detective scrutinizing every detail, from nervous fidgeting to subtle changes in tone of voice, to uncover hidden truths.

- **Example:** An investigator questioning a suspect observes them avoiding eye contact and fidgeting excessively. These nonverbal cues might be interpreted as signs of deception, prompting further investigation.

2. Interrogation Techniques: The ability to elicit information was crucial. Arthashastra mentions various methods, including using deception, playing on the suspect's emotions, and offering incentives for truthful confessions. However, Dharmashastras, the legal texts, emphasized ethical treatment of suspects.

- **Example:** An investigator facing a tight-lipped witness might offer a reward for any information that leads to solving the case. This could encourage the witness to come forward with what they know.

3. The Power of Disguise: Going undercover was a valuable tool. Investigators might disguise themselves as merchants, mendicants, or even members of the opposing party to infiltrate groups and gather information.

- **Example:** An investigator suspects a conspiracy within the royal court. They might disguise themselves as a new servant to gain access to private conversations and observe the interactions between potential suspects.

4. Witness Testimony: Eyewitness accounts were a cornerstone of investigations. Dharmashastras established guidelines for evaluating witness credibility, considering factors like social status, potential biases, and the consistency of their statements.

- **Example:** Investigators might interview multiple witnesses to a crime, comparing their accounts for discrepancies or inconsistencies. A witness with a known grudge against the suspect might have their testimony viewed with more skepticism.

5. Ordeals by Fire or Water: These were controversial practices mentioned in some ancient texts. The accused would be subjected to a potentially dangerous ordeal, with the belief that divine intervention would protect the innocent. However, these methods were not universally accepted and faced criticism for being unreliable and barbaric.

It's important to note that the historical accuracy and ethical implications of some of these practices are debated. However, they offer a window into the ingenuity and resourcefulness of ancient Indian investigators who, despite lacking modern technology, developed a system for uncovering the truth and upholding justice.

Bonus: Fingerprints - A Timeless Tool: Interestingly, ancient India recognized the uniqueness of fingerprints. The Samudra Shastra, a Hindu scripture, mentions 12 different fingerprint patterns. While not used for identification in the same way as modern forensics, this recognition of individuality demonstrates the keen observation skills of ancient investigators.

CHAPTER FOUR

Investigating a Changing Landscape: Techniques in Medieval and Colonial India

The art of investigation in India evolved significantly during the medieval and colonial periods. Here's how:

The Mughal Era: Maintaining Order

- **The Daroga's Duty:** The Mughal Empire saw the rise of the daroga, a local police officer responsible for maintaining order and investigating crimes. They relied on a network of informers and witnesses to gather information.
- **Example:** A daroga investigating a theft in the marketplace might question nearby shopkeepers and passersby, piecing together details about the suspect's appearance and escape route based on eyewitness accounts.
- **Focus on Public Order:** Investigations during this period often focused on crimes that disrupted public

order, such as theft, robbery, and violence. Political crimes and offenses against the state might be handled by a separate investigative branch.

The Colonial Era: A New System Emerges

- **The British Influence:** The arrival of the British East India Company brought significant changes to the investigative landscape. They implemented a more centralized police system, establishing police stations (thanas) and appointing thana darogas as officers.
- **Thanedar’s Toolkit:** The thana daroga might utilize a variety of methods, including witness interrogation, gathering circumstantial evidence, and potentially even rudimentary forensic techniques like footprint analysis.
- **Thaggee Challenges:** A significant challenge of the colonial era was Thaggee, a network of organized crime specializing in highway robbery and murder. Investigations often involved tracking down these elusive criminals, infiltrating their networks through undercover agents, and using captured informants to gather intelligence.
- **Early Forensics:** While not as sophisticated as modern methods, the colonial period saw the beginnings of forensic investigation. Fingerprint identification, though not yet a widespread practice, was explored by some British officials in India. Footprint analysis and examination of physical evidence at crime scenes were also employed to some extent.

Limitations and Biases: It’s important to acknowledge the limitations of these systems. Colonial era investigations were often biased towards protecting British interests, and the rights of suspects were not always upheld. However, the introduction of a more structured police force and some early forensic practices laid the groundwork for the development of a more modern investigative system in India.

A Legacy of Adaptation: The medieval and colonial periods in India showcase the constant evolution of investigative techniques. From the reliance on informers and witness testimony to the beginnings of forensics, these eras demonstrate the continuous efforts to adapt investigative methods to the challenges of the times. These historical practices inform our understanding of the development of the modern Indian investigative system.

CHAPTER FIVE

Unveiling the Truth in a Modern Nation: Investigations in Post-Independence India

India's independence in 1947 ushered in a new era of investigative practices. Here's how the landscape transformed:

The Rise of the IPS:

- **Professionalism Takes Center Stage:** The Indian Police Service (IPS) was established, emphasizing rigorous training and professional conduct for investigators. This marked a shift from the less standardized practices of the colonial era.
- **Example:** An IPS officer investigating a financial crime has undergone extensive training in financial forensics, allowing them to analyze bank records, identify

suspicious transactions, and build a strong case against the suspect.

CIDs: Tackling Complex Crimes:

- **Specialization for Serious Cases:** Criminal Investigation Departments (CIDs) were established within various states. These specialized units handle complex investigations like homicides, organized crime, and cybercrime.
- **Example:** A CID team investigating a serial murder case utilizes advanced profiling techniques, crime scene analysis, and collaboration with forensic experts to identify and apprehend the culprit. They might also work with other state CIDs or central investigative agencies if the case has national implications.

The Power of Forensics:

- **Science in the Service of Justice:** Forensic science gained prominence. State-of-the-art laboratories analyze fingerprints, ballistics (firearm evidence), DNA samples, and other physical evidence to strengthen investigations.
- **Example:** Investigators recover a fingerprint from a crime scene. The fingerprint is analyzed by a forensic laboratory, leading to a match with a known criminal in a national database. This crucial piece of evidence helps build a strong case against the suspect.
- **Technological Advancements:** The modern investigator's toolkit extends beyond traditional methods. Digital forensics helps examine electronic devices for evidence, and DNA analysis can link

suspects to a crime scene with unparalleled accuracy. Cybercrime investigations rely on expertise in tracing online activity and uncovering digital footprints.

Collaboration is Key:

- **A Network of Expertise:** Modern investigations often involve collaboration between different agencies. The IPS, CIDs, and forensic labs work together, and sometimes even federal investigative agencies like the Central Bureau of Investigation (CBI) get involved in complex cases. This combined effort increases the chances of a successful investigation.
- **Example:** A terror attack investigation might involve the CID, forensic teams specializing in explosives analysis, and the National Investigation Agency (NIA) which focuses on counter-terrorism. Information sharing and coordinated efforts across agencies ensure a comprehensive investigation.

The Ever-Evolving Landscape:

The world of investigations in India is constantly evolving. New technologies emerge, and criminal methods become more sophisticated. The modern investigator must be adaptable, continuously learning new skills and staying updated on the latest advancements to remain effective in the face of ever-changing challenges.

Building on a Legacy: Post-independence India's investigative system combines the best aspects of professional training, specialized units, and cutting-edge forensic science. This approach ensures that investigations are conducted with professionalism, utilize the power of science, and ultimately strive to deliver justice.

The Investigator's Skillset

- Chapter 7: The Investigator’s Sharp Mind: Analytical Thinking in Indian Private Investigations
- Chapter 8: The Keen Eye: Attention to Detail in Indian Private Investigations
- Chapter 9: The Power of Words: Communication Skills in Indian Private Investigations
- Chapter 10: The Trusted Shadow: Discretion and Confidentiality in Indian Private Investigations
- Chapter 11: The Art of Adjustment: Adaptability in Indian Private Investigations
- Chapter 12: The Long Game: Persistence and Patience in Indian Private Investigations
- Chapter 15: The Heart of the Matter: Empathy and Interpersonal Skills in Indian Private Investigations
- Chapter 16 (duplicate): The Demands of the Job: Staying Healthy (This chapter might be better placed under Part 5: Professional Development)

CHAPTER SIX

The Investigator's Sharp Mind: Analytical Thinking in Private Investigations

The hallmark of a skilled private investigator in India is a sharp analytical mind. Here's how investigators cultivate this crucial skill:

1. **Critical Thinking:** At the core lies critical thinking – the ability to analyze information objectively and identify its strengths and weaknesses. Investigators must question assumptions, consider all perspectives, and avoid jumping to conclusions.
2. **Pattern Recognition:** A keen eye for patterns is essential. Investigators sift through mountains of data, witness accounts, and evidence, searching for connections and recurring themes. Identifying patterns in seemingly unrelated details can be a breakthrough in an investigation.

3. **Logical Reasoning:** Once patterns emerge, the investigator needs to apply logical reasoning to draw conclusions. This involves using evidence and established facts to build a logical chain of events that explains the situation.
4. **Assessing Evidence:** Evaluating evidence is a crucial skill. Investigators must assess the credibility of sources, consider the context in which evidence was collected, and weigh the strength of different pieces of evidence.
5. **Identifying Inconsistencies:** Inconsistencies in witness accounts, alibis, or financial records can be crucial clues. Investigators must be adept at spotting these inconsistencies and determining if they are minor errors or point towards something more significant.
6. **Open-mindedness:** While a strong analytical mind is key, investigators also need to be open-minded. New evidence or information can emerge at any point, requiring them to adapt their analysis and adjust their conclusions accordingly.

The Art of Deduction: Developing an analytical mindset is an ongoing process for private investigators. Through experience and honing critical thinking skills, they become adept at dissecting complex situations, connecting the dots, and drawing logical conclusions based on the evidence. This analytical prowess is what allows them to crack the case and deliver the truth to their clients.

CHAPTER SEVEN

The Keen Eye: Attention to Detail in Investigations

For a private investigator in India, a meticulous eye for detail is an essential tool. Here's why:

1. **Unearthing Clues:** Investigations are often built upon a foundation of seemingly insignificant details. A misplaced receipt, an unusual mark on a document, or a fleeting change in someone's behavior – these can all be crucial clues if noticed. A keen eye for detail allows investigators to spot these potential leads and follow them up.
2. **Scrutinizing Evidence:** Once evidence is collected, it needs thorough scrutiny. This could involve examining documents for inconsistencies, analyzing surveillance footage for subtle details, or even picking up on nuances in witness statements. A detail-oriented approach ensures investigators don't miss any vital piece of information.

3. **Verification and Accuracy:** In the world of investigations, accuracy is paramount. Investigators need to verify all information obtained, cross-reference details, and ensure their findings are based on solid evidence. Attention to detail minimizes the risk of errors and ensures the investigation is built on a foundation of factual accuracy.
4. **Following the Paper Trail:** Many investigations involve a paper trail – financial records, property ownership documents, or communication logs. A meticulous investigator can follow this trail, piecing together information and identifying discrepancies or suspicious patterns. Attention to detail is key to unearthing the truth hidden within the paperwork.
5. **Observation Skills:** Surveillance is a common investigative technique. Investigators need keen observation skills to pick up on subtle cues – body language, interactions with others, or deviations from routine behavior. A detail-oriented approach allows them to gather valuable information from their observations.

The Art of Seeing: Attention to detail is not just about spotting things; it's about understanding their significance. By cultivating a meticulous eye, private investigators can transform seemingly insignificant details into valuable leads, ultimately leading them closer to the truth.

CHAPTER EIGHT

The Power of Words: Communication Skills in Private Investigations

The success of an investigation often hinges on the investigator's communication skills. Here's how private investigators in India leverage their communication prowess:

1. **Active Listening:** At the heart of effective communication lies active listening. Investigators need to pay close attention to what witnesses and clients are saying, not just the words themselves, but also the underlying emotions and unspoken details. Active listening fosters trust and encourages people to share information freely.
2. **Building Rapport:** Establishing rapport is crucial, especially when interviewing witnesses or dealing with potentially apprehensive clients. Investigators achieve this through open body language, genuine interest, and

clear communication of their purpose and methods. A good rapport puts people at ease and encourages them to be more forthcoming.

3. **Clear and Concise Communication:** Investigators need to articulate themselves clearly and concisely, both verbally and in writing. This involves avoiding jargon or overly technical terms, ensuring their message is understood by everyone involved. Clarity is essential for gathering accurate information from witnesses and for presenting findings to clients in a way that is easy to comprehend.
4. **Adapting Communication Style:** A skilled investigator can adapt their communication style to the situation and the person they are interacting with. With a nervous witness, they might use a more empathetic and reassuring approach, while with a client, they might adopt a more professional and direct tone. This adaptability fosters trust and ensures effective communication across different scenarios.
5. **Written Communication:** Strong writing skills are essential for crafting comprehensive reports. Investigators need to present their findings in a clear, organized, and objective manner. The report should be free of grammatical errors and easy to read, even for someone without a legal background.

The Art of Conversation: Effective communication is a two-way street. By actively listening, building rapport, and expressing themselves clearly, private investigators can gather crucial information, build trust with clients, and ultimately deliver a successful investigation.

CHAPTER NINE

The Trusted Shadow: Discretion and Confidentiality in Private Investigations

The world of private investigations thrives on secrecy. Here's how investigators in India navigate the delicate balance of discretion and confidentiality:

1. **Client Trust is Paramount:** Clients entrust private investigators with highly sensitive information. Maintaining confidentiality is paramount. This means keeping client details, the nature of the investigation, and any collected evidence strictly confidential. A breach of confidentiality can damage the client's reputation or even put them at risk.
2. **Discretion in Every Step:** Discretion goes beyond just information security. It's about maintaining a low profile throughout the investigation. Investigators should avoid drawing unnecessary attention to themselves or the client's situation. This includes being

mindful of their actions in public and keeping conversations about the case private.

3. **Selective Information Sharing:** Investigators need to be selective about who they share information with. They should only disclose details on a need-to-know basis, keeping the circle of those aware of the investigation as small as possible.
4. **Legal and Ethical Obligations:** Confidentiality is not just about protecting the client; it's also a legal and ethical obligation. Investigators are bound by professional codes and may face legal repercussions for breaching confidentiality.
5. **Maintaining Professional Distance:** Developing a professional rapport with clients is important, but investigators should avoid becoming overly involved in the emotional aspects of the case. Maintaining a sense of professional distance allows them to focus on the investigation objectively and prioritize confidentiality.

Building Trust Through Secrecy: Discretion and confidentiality are the cornerstones of trust in private investigations. By adhering to these principles, investigators build strong relationships with their clients and ensure that sensitive information remains secure throughout the investigation process.

CHAPTER TEN

The Art of Adjustment: Adaptability in Private Investigations

The world of private investigations is rarely a smooth ride. Here's how investigators in India navigate the unexpected with adaptability:

Thinking on Their Feet: No two cases are identical. Investigators encounter unforeseen challenges, from uncooperative witnesses to sudden changes in the subject's behavior. Adaptability allows them to adjust their approach on the fly, devising new strategies to gather information or overcome roadblocks.

- **Example:** An investigator following a suspect notices them entering a restricted building. The original plan for discreet tailing might need to be scrapped. The investigator might need to adapt, finding a way to track the suspect's movements without compromising their cover or resorting to illegal methods.

Embracing New Technology: The world of investigations is constantly evolving, with new technologies emerging all the time. A successful investigator is open to learning and adapting to these advancements. This could involve using social media for background checks, drone technology for surveillance in remote areas, or data analysis tools for sifting through large amounts of digital information.

- **Example:** A pre-marital investigation involves verifying the potential spouse's social media activity. The investigator, familiar with social media verification techniques, can use them to identify fake profiles or uncover inconsistencies in the subject's online persona.

Shifting Gears Mid-Investigation: As investigations unfold, new information or evidence can come to light, necessitating a change in course. Adaptable investigators can analyze this new information, adjust their hypothesis, and modify their investigative approach accordingly.

- **Example:** A missing person case initially focuses on a runaway scenario. However, a witness comes forward with details suggesting foul play. The investigator needs to adapt, shifting their focus to potential abduction or other criminal activity, tailoring their investigation to gather evidence that supports this new direction.

Cultural Sensitivity: India is a diverse country with a rich tapestry of cultures. A skilled investigator demonstrates cultural sensitivity, understanding and respecting local customs and traditions. This allows them to build rapport with people from different backgrounds and navigate potentially challenging situations effectively.

- **Example:** An investigator conducting an investigation in a rural village needs to be mindful of local customs and dress modestly. They might also need to work with a translator to ensure clear communication with witnesses who speak a different language.

The Investigator as a Chameleon: Adaptability is a hallmark of a successful private investigator. By thinking on their feet, embracing new tools, adjusting their approach, and demonstrating cultural sensitivity, investigators can navigate the unexpected twists and turns of a case, ultimately achieving their goals and uncovering the truth.

CHAPTER ELEVEN

The Long Game: Persistence and Patience in Private Investigations

The world of private investigations isn't always about thrilling chases and dramatic breakthroughs. Here's how investigators in India cultivate the crucial skills of persistence and patience:

Following the Faint Trail: Investigations rarely unfold in a linear fashion. Leads can be dead ends, witnesses might be uncooperative, and progress can feel agonizingly slow. Persistence is key – the relentless pursuit of answers, even when the trail seems cold.

- **Example:** A missing person case with few leads. The investigator persistently follows up on every possible sighting, examines public records thoroughly, and tirelessly interviews anyone who might have even a shred of information. This unwavering pursuit can eventually lead to a crucial breakthrough.

Patience is a Virtue: Investigations take time. Building trust with witnesses, gathering evidence through legal means, and analyzing information all require patience. A hasty investigator might miss crucial details or jump to inaccurate conclusions.

- **Example:** An investigator conducting surveillance on a suspected embezzler needs to be patient. Gathering enough concrete evidence to build a strong case might involve waiting for the suspect to make a mistake, which could take days or even weeks.

Undeterred by Setbacks: Setbacks are inevitable. Witnesses might retract statements, leads might go nowhere, and new information might contradict initial assumptions. A persistent investigator doesn't give up easily. They analyze setbacks, adjust their approach, and continue their pursuit of the truth.

- **Example:** An investigator following a money trail encounters a dead end – a seemingly clean bank account. Persistence might lead them to investigate the account holder's associates or delve deeper into financial records, eventually uncovering hidden transactions that expose the truth.

The Marathon, Not the Sprint: Successful private investigations are marathons, not sprints. Persistence and patience are the fuel that keeps investigators going. By relentlessly following leads, waiting for the right moment, and remaining undeterred by setbacks, investigators can crack even the most challenging cases and deliver results for their clients.

CHAPTER TWELVE

The Heart of the Matter: Empathy and Interpersonal Skills in Private Investigations

The image of a private investigator might conjure visions of a lone wolf, coldly gathering facts. But the reality is far more nuanced. Success in Indian private investigations hinges on strong empathy and interpersonal skills. Here's why:

- **Understanding the Human Cost:** Investigations often deal with sensitive situations – missing loved ones, infidelity, or financial ruin. A skilled investigator possesses empathy, the ability to understand and share the feelings of those involved. They can listen attentively, acknowledge their pain, and approach the case with a sense of compassion. Imagine a doctor treating a patient – their technical skills are crucial, but so is their bedside manner, which in this case translates to emotional understanding.

- **Example:** An investigator meets with a distraught family who has hired them to find a missing child. The investigator doesn't just focus on gathering facts; they acknowledge the family's fear and anxiety, offering words of comfort and reassurance while remaining professional and focused on the task at hand.
- **Building Bridges, Not Walls:** Investigations require interaction with a diverse range of people – worried clients, hesitant witnesses, or even evasive subjects. Strong interpersonal skills are essential for building rapport and fostering trust. This involves active listening, clear communication, and the ability to put people at ease. Imagine a diplomat navigating a complex negotiation – they need to be firm yet respectful, finding common ground to move forward.
- **Example:** An investigator interviews a witness who might be apprehensive about coming forward. The investigator uses their interpersonal skills to create a safe and comfortable space, demonstrating empathy for the witness's concerns and explaining the importance of their testimony. This is like building a bridge of trust, allowing the witness to feel comfortable sharing what they know.
- **Disarming Suspects (Verbally, Not Literally):** While private investigators aren't law enforcement, they may need to interact with potential suspects. Here, empathy can be a powerful tool. By acknowledging the suspect's perspective and demonstrating a willingness to listen without judgment, an investigator might be able to elicit information that would otherwise be withheld. Imagine a chess player anticipating their opponent's moves – the investigator uses empathy to understand the suspect's motivations and tailor their approach accordingly.

- **Example:** An investigator confronts a suspected embezzler. Instead of taking an accusatory tone, they use empathy to explore the reasons behind the suspect's actions. This approach might lead to a confession or a willingness to cooperate, potentially leading to a quicker resolution of the case.

The Power of Connection: Empathy and interpersonal skills are not soft skills; they are the cornerstones of successful private investigations in India. By understanding the human element of each case and building genuine connections with those involved, investigators navigate emotional complexities, gather crucial information, and ultimately deliver results for their clients.

CHAPTER THIRTEEN

The Demands of the Job: Being Fit

- **Long Hours and Unpredictable Schedules:** Investigations rarely follow a 9-to-5 routine. Stakeouts, chasing leads, and interviewing witnesses can involve extended periods on the job, demanding stamina and physical resilience.
- **Physical Activity:** Surveillance often involves following subjects on foot, climbing stairs, or navigating challenging terrain. Good physical fitness allows investigators to keep up and maintain discreet observation.
- **Stressful Situations:** Investigations can be emotionally draining, dealing with sensitive topics and facing potential danger. Physical fitness can contribute to overall well-being and better stress management.

The Advantages of Being Healthy and Fit:

- **Enhanced Stamina:** Good stamina allows investigators to maintain focus and effectiveness during long stakeouts or physically demanding situations. They can keep up with their subjects without compromising the investigation.

- **Improved Agility and Reflexes:** Physical fitness can enhance reflexes and agility, which can be beneficial in unexpected situations. Imagine needing to chase down a fleeing suspect – good reflexes and agility can make all the difference.
- **Reduced Risk of Injury:** The job can involve physical risks like slips, falls, or even minor altercations. Being physically fit reduces the chances of injuries and allows for quicker recovery if they do occur.
- **Increased Mental Toughness:** Maintaining physical health often goes hand-in-hand with mental resilience. A healthy investigator is better equipped to handle the demanding work hours, unpredictable situations, and emotional challenges inherent to the job.

Maintaining Physical Fitness:

- **Regular Exercise:** Engaging in regular exercise, like running, swimming, or weight training, improves stamina, strength, and overall fitness.
- **Healthy Diet:** A balanced diet provides the body with the fuel it needs to perform at its best. Proper nutrition enhances energy levels and promotes overall well-being.
- **Adequate Sleep:** Sufficient sleep is crucial for both physical and mental recovery. A well-rested investigator is more alert, focused, and ready to tackle the challenges of the job.

Health and Fitness: A Competitive Advantage:

In the competitive world of private investigations, physical fitness can be a significant advantage. It allows investigators to handle demanding situations, work long hours, and maintain a sharp focus. It's not just about physical capabilities; good health contributes to mental well-being and overall resilience, making a private investigator a more effective and reliable professional.

The Investigative Process

- Chapter 14: Securing the Clues: A Guide to Evidence Collection in India
- Chapter 15: Cracking the Code: Analysis and Interpretation in Indian Investigations
- Chapter 16: Putting it All Together: Report Writing in Indian Private Investigations
- Chapter 17: Shadow Play: Unveiling the Truth with Surveillance Investigations
- Chapter 18: Sifting Through the Past: Background Checks and Due Diligence
- Chapter 19: Safeguarding the Enterprise: Unveiling the Truths Behind Corporate Investigations
- Chapter 20: Unveiling the Truth: Insurance Investigations
- Chapter 21: The Unsung Heroes: Legal Support Services in Action
- Chapter 22: Finding the Lost: Unveiling the Strategies of Missing Persons Investigations
- Chapter 23: Following the Money Trail: Unveiling the Truth with Financial Investigations
- Chapter 24: Navigating the Digital Wild West: Unveiling Cyber Crimes with Cyber Investigations
- Chapter 25: Crime Scene: A meticulous dance to secure the truth (This chapter could be renamed "Securing the Scene" for better flow)
- Chapter 26: The Paper Trail: Documenting the Undisclosed Story

CHAPTER FOURTEEN

Securing the Clues: A Guide to Evidence Collection in India

Unearthing the truth hinges on strong evidence. Here's how investigators in India approach evidence collection, following legal guidelines:

1. **Identifying Relevant Evidence:** The first step involves understanding the case and pinpointing what kind of evidence would be most helpful. This could be:
    - **Physical Evidence:** Tangible objects found at the scene, like fingerprints, weapons, or CCTV footage.
        - **Example:** In a theft case, investigators might collect fingerprints from the scene of the crime or stolen goods found in the suspect's possession.
    - **Testimonial Evidence:** Statements from witnesses who have firsthand information about the case.

        - **Example:** Witness accounts can be crucial in accident investigations or situations where a crime occurred in public view.

    - **Electronic Evidence:** Digital records like emails, phone records, or social media posts that can shed light on the case.

        - **Example:** In a case of financial fraud, investigators might analyze bank transactions or email exchanges to track the movement of funds.

2. **Preserving the Evidence:** Once identified, the evidence needs to be carefully collected and preserved to avoid contamination or loss. This might involve using proper techniques for fingerprint lifting, following the chain of custody for physical objects, and ensuring digital records are securely stored.
3. **Legal Considerations:** Indian law dictates how evidence can be obtained. Private investigators cannot violate anyone's privacy or break the law to gather evidence. They rely on legal methods like witness interviews with consent or obtaining court orders for accessing certain electronic records.
4. **Documentation:** Throughout the process, meticulous documentation is essential. This includes maintaining a record of when and where evidence was collected, following a chain of custody to track its movement, and noting any observations made during collection.

Remember: Evidence collection is a crucial step in any investigation. By following these guidelines and adhering to legal boundaries, investigators ensure the evidence they gather is admissible in court and strengthens the case.

CHAPTER FIFTEEN

Cracking the Code: Analysis and Interpretation in Investigations

Once the investigative net has gathered its haul, the true magic happens – analysis and interpretation. Here's how private investigators in India sift through the evidence to find the truth:

1. **Scrutinizing the Pieces:** The investigator meticulously examines all collected evidence – witness statements, physical objects, and digital records. This involves close reading, identifying key details, and looking for inconsistencies or contradictions.
2. **Pattern Recognition:** The focus then shifts to identifying patterns and connections between different pieces of evidence. For example, inconsistencies in witness accounts or unusual activity in financial records might point towards something amiss.

3. **Bridging the Gaps:** Inevitably, investigations might have gaps in information. The investigator will consider these gaps and try to determine if they are critical to the case. They might then strategize ways to gather additional information to fill those gaps, if possible.
4. **Hypothesis Formation:** Based on the analysis, the investigator formulates a hypothesis – a plausible explanation for what happened. This hypothesis should consider all the collected evidence and address any identified patterns or inconsistencies.
5. **Testing the Hypothesis:** The investigator doesn't simply accept the initial hypothesis. They test it against new information or by seeking additional evidence to corroborate or refute it. This ensures a well-rounded understanding of the case.
6. **Drawing Conclusions:** When the analysis is complete and the hypothesis is well-supported by evidence, the investigator can arrive at a conclusion. This conclusion should be objective, based solely on the facts and avoiding any personal biases.

Scientific Conviction, Legal Constraints: While scientific methods guide the analysis, private investigators in India operate within legal boundaries. Their conclusions cannot be presented as absolute truths but rather as strong possibilities backed by the gathered evidence. The investigator's role is to present a clear picture to the client, allowing them to make informed decisions based on the findings.

CHAPTER SIXTEEN

Putting it All Together: Report Writing in Private Investigations

The culmination of any investigation is a well-crafted report that delivers the findings. Here's how private investigators in India translate their detective work into a clear and concise document:

1. **Compiling the Findings:** After meticulous analysis and interpretation, the investigator gathers all the information – notes, evidence, and conclusions – to structure the report.
2. **Crafting the Narrative:** The report is essentially a story, but one built on facts. The investigator structures it with clear sections:

    - **Executive Summary:** A concise overview of the case, including the client's concerns, the investigation conducted, and the key findings.
    - **Background:** This section provides context, outlining the situation that led to the investigation

and any relevant details about the involved parties.

- **Investigation Process:** Here, the investigator details the steps taken during the investigation. This might include methods used for gathering evidence, like witness interviews or surveillance activities (always adhering to legal boundaries).
- **Evidence:** This is the heart of the report, presenting all the collected evidence in a clear and organized manner. Physical evidence might be described with photos or sketches, while witness statements are summarized and inconsistencies highlighted. Digital evidence might be presented in screenshots or reports depending on its nature.
- **Conclusions:** This section provides the investigator's objective assessment of the situation based on the analysis of the evidence. It should avoid personal opinions and focus on presenting a logical conclusion based on the facts.
- **Recommendations:** Depending on the case, the investigator might offer recommendations for next steps. This could involve suggestions for the client on how to proceed or further actions that could be taken based on the findings (always within legal boundaries).

3. **Clarity and Concision:** The report should be written in clear, concise language, avoiding legal jargon or overly technical terms. It should be easy for the client to understand, even if they don't have a legal background.
4. **Objectivity and Accuracy:** The report is a factual document. The investigator should avoid personal opinions or biases, focusing solely on presenting the evidence and its interpretation in an objective manner.

Accuracy is paramount, ensuring all details and evidence are presented correctly.

The Final Chapter: A well-written report is the investigator's final contribution to the case. It serves as a permanent record of the investigation and its findings, providing a clear picture for the client and potentially serving as evidence in legal proceedings, if applicable.

CHAPTER SEVENTEEN

Shadow Play: Unveiling the Truth with Surveillance Investigations

Surveillance investigations are a discreet method for gathering crucial information. They involve monitoring a person, place, or activity to uncover hidden truths. Here's a breakdown of their purpose, use cases, and methods:

Unmasking the Motive: The Purpose of Surveillance

The primary purpose of a surveillance investigation is to gather information that would otherwise be difficult or impossible to obtain through conventional means. Investigators use discreet observation to:

- **Document Activities:** They meticulously record the subject's actions, movements, and interactions with others. This data can be used to build a timeline of events and identify potential leads.
- **Example:** A spouse suspects infidelity. A surveillance investigator might discreetly follow the suspected

partner, documenting their movements and interactions with another person.

- **Gather Evidence:** Surveillance can capture concrete evidence to support or refute allegations. Video recordings of suspicious activity or interactions can be used as evidence in court proceedings.
- **Example:** An insurance company suspects a client is filing a fraudulent disability claim. Surveillance might reveal the client engaging in activities inconsistent with their claimed limitations.

Real-World Applications: Use Cases for Surveillance

Surveillance investigations are employed across various scenarios where discreet observation is vital:

- **Infidelity Cases:** As in the example above, surveillance can help a spouse determine if their partner is indeed engaging in extramarital affairs.
- **Insurance Fraud:** Surveillance helps insurance companies investigate suspicious claims. For instance, an individual claiming back injuries might be caught on video engaging in strenuous activities.
- **Employee Misconduct:** Companies may utilize surveillance to investigate suspected employee theft, misuse of company property, or violation of company policies.
- **Example:** A company suspects an employee of stealing from the warehouse after hours. Surveillance cameras strategically placed might capture the employee's suspicious activity.
- **Missing Persons:** In some cases, surveillance can be used to locate missing individuals. This could involve monitoring known haunts of the missing person or

following up on leads gathered from witnesses.

Tools of the Trade: Methods for Discreet Observation

Surveillance investigators employ various methods to maintain a low profile while gathering information. Here are some common techniques:

- **Physical Surveillance:** Investigators follow the subject on foot or by vehicle, maintaining a safe distance while discreetly observing their activities.
- **Vehicle Tracking:** GPS trackers can be placed on a vehicle to monitor its movements and pinpoint the subject's location.
- **Video and Photo Documentation:** Covertly capturing video or photographs of the subject's activities can provide concrete evidence to support suspicions.

Ethical Considerations:

It's crucial to note that surveillance investigations must adhere to legal and ethical guidelines. Trespassing, illegal wiretapping, and privacy violations are strictly prohibited. A reputable investigation firm will only conduct surveillance within the bounds of the law and with proper authorization when necessary.

Conclusion:

Surveillance investigations, when conducted ethically and legally, can be a powerful tool for uncovering the truth. By employing various methods of discreet observation, investigators can gather vital information that sheds light on hidden activities and helps resolve complex situations.

CHAPTER EIGHTEEN

Sifting Through the Past: Background Checks and Due Diligence

Making informed decisions often hinges on knowing who you're dealing with. Background checks and due diligence investigations provide a comprehensive overview of an individual's or entity's history and reputation. Let's delve into their purpose, use cases, and the methods employed to gather information.

Unveiling the Past: The Purpose of Background Checks and Due Diligence

Both background checks and due diligence aim to verify information provided by an individual or entity. They achieve this by:

- **Verifying Identity:** Confirming the person's name, address, Social Security number, and other identifying details are accurate and legitimate.

- **Investigating History:** Unearthing past criminal records, employment history, education credentials, and potential financial issues.
- **Assessing Reputation:** Evaluating the individual's or entity's reputation through reference checks, news articles, and online reviews.

When Knowledge is Power: Use Cases for Background Checks and Due Diligence

These investigations play a crucial role in various situations where trust and reliability are paramount:

- **Pre-Employment Screening:** Employers use background checks to verify an applicant's qualifications, identify potential red flags like criminal history or employment gaps, and ensure they are hiring someone who aligns with the company's values.
- **Example:** A company conducting a background check on a potential financial advisor might uncover past regulatory violations or financial misconduct, leading them to reconsider the candidate.
- **Tenant Checks:** Landlords utilize background checks to assess a potential tenant's creditworthiness, rental history, and criminal background to minimize the risk of property damage or non-payment of rent.

- **Example:** A background checks reveals a potential tenant has a history of evictions due to non-payment. This information helps the landlord make an informed decision about renting the property.
- **Business Partnerships:** Before entering a business partnership, due diligence is crucial. This involves investigating the potential partner's financial health,

legal history, and reputation within the industry.

- **Example:** A company considering a merger with another firm might conduct due diligence to uncover any hidden liabilities or potential legal issues associated with the target company.

Methods for Meticulous Research:

Background checks and due diligence investigations rely on various methods to gather information:

- **Public Record Searches:** Investigators access databases of criminal records, court filings, bankruptcy proceedings, and professional licenses.
- **Reference Checks:** Contacting past employers, colleagues, or landlords to verify information provided by the subject and gain insights into their work ethic, character, and reliability.
- **Financial Data Analysis:** Examining credit reports, tax liens, and other financial documents to assess the individual's or entity's financial stability and identify potential liabilities.
- **Online Investigations:** Searching for information about the subject online, including social media profiles, news articles, and public forums, to gain a broader picture of their reputation and past activities.

Privacy and Legal Considerations:

It's important to conduct background checks and due diligence investigations within legal boundaries. Fair Credit Reporting Act (FCRA) regulations govern the use of consumer credit reports for pre-employment screening purposes. Always obtain consent from the subject before initiating a background check, and ensure the information gathered is used for legitimate purposes.

The Power of Information:

By providing a comprehensive picture of an individual's or entity's background and reputation, background checks and due diligence investigations empower informed decision-making. These practices help mitigate risks, ensure trust in professional relationships, and ultimately contribute to more successful ventures and safer communities.

CHAPTER NINETEEN

Safeguarding the Enterprise: Unveiling the Truths Behind Corporate Investigations

The corporate world thrives on trust and transparency. But when suspicion arises, corporate investigations become essential to protect a company's well-being. Here's a closer look at their purpose, the situations that necessitate them, and the methods investigators employ to uncover the truth.

Guarding the Castle: The Purpose of Corporate Investigations

Corporate investigations aim to identify and address wrongdoing within an organization. Their primary goals are to:

- **Protect Company Assets:** Investigate and prevent internal fraud, embezzlement, or misuse of company resources.

- **Safeguard Intellectual Property:** Uncover and address instances of intellectual property theft, such as trade secrets being leaked to competitors.
- **Maintain a Positive Reputation:** Investigate allegations of misconduct or unethical behavior that could damage the company's public image.
- **Uphold Compliance:** Ensure the company adheres to all relevant laws and regulations.

When Whispers Turn Serious: Use Cases for Corporate Investigations

Several situations can trigger the need for a corporate investigation:

- **Financial Discrepancies:** Unexplained fluctuations in financial records, missing inventory, or discrepancies in expense reports might indicate embezzlement or internal fraud.
- **Example:** An accounting department flags a series of unusual purchases made by a mid-level manager. A corporate investigation might reveal the manager has been creating fake vendors and pocketing the company funds.
- **Intellectual Property Concerns:** A competitor launches a product suspiciously similar to a company's proprietary design. An investigation can determine if there has been a breach of intellectual property rights.
- **Example:** A software company suspects a disgruntled ex-employee leaked confidential source code to a rival firm. A digital forensics investigation can analyze the ex-employee's computer and company network to identify any potential data breaches.

- **Workplace Misconduct:** Allegations of sexual harassment, discrimination, or workplace violence require a thorough investigation to ensure a safe and ethical work environment.
- **Example:** An employee anonymously reports a supervisor engaging in bullying behavior. A corporate investigation can interview witnesses and gather evidence to determine the truth behind the allegations.

Tools of the Trade: Methods Used in Corporate Investigations

Corporate investigators utilize a variety of methods to gather information and uncover wrongdoing:

- **Forensic Accounting:** Forensic accountants analyze financial records to identify patterns of fraud, embezzlement, or misuse of funds.
- **Undercover Work:** In some cases, undercover investigators may be deployed to infiltrate suspected fraudulent activities or gather information from within the company.
- **Digital Forensics:** Examining company computers, servers, and electronic devices can reveal deleted emails, hidden files, and other digital footprints that can be crucial evidence.
- **Employee Interviews:** Skilled investigators conduct confidential interviews with employees to gather information and identify potential witnesses.
- **Public Record Searches:** Investigating the backgrounds of individuals involved in suspicious activities can reveal relevant information about their past.

Confidentiality and Legal Considerations:

Corporate investigations must be conducted with utmost confidentiality to avoid damaging the company's reputation or jeopardizing ongoing legal proceedings. Investigators must comply with all relevant data privacy laws and regulations when gathering information.

Protecting the Company's Future:

Corporate investigations play a critical role in safeguarding a company's assets, reputation, and future success. By employing a variety of investigative methods and adhering to ethical and legal guidelines, companies can identify and address wrongdoing, maintain a culture of integrity, and build trust with stakeholders.

CHAPTER TWENTY

Unveiling the Truth: Insurance Investigations

Insurance companies rely on investigations to ensure the validity of claims. These investigations aim to separate legitimate claims from fraudulent ones, protecting the company's resources and ensuring fair premiums for honest customers. Let's delve into the purpose, use cases, and methods employed in insurance investigations.

Safeguarding Resources: The Purpose of Insurance Investigations

Insurance investigations serve two primary purposes:

- **Combatting Fraud:** Identifying and preventing fraudulent claims that can cost insurance companies billions of dollars annually. This protects honest policyholders from bearing the burden of inflated premiums.
- **Ensuring Fairness:** Verifying the legitimacy of claims ensures that those who suffer genuine losses receive the compensation they deserve.

Suspicious Situations: Use Cases for Insurance Investigations

Insurance investigations are triggered by red flags that raise doubts about the validity of a claim:

- **Auto Accidents:** Claims with inconsistencies in the reported details, suspicious injuries, or potential staged accidents might warrant investigation.
- **Example:** An insurance company investigates a car accident claim where the reported damage to the vehicles seems excessive compared to the alleged speed and impact of the collision.
- **Disability Claims:** Claims for disability benefits based on injuries or illnesses that don't seem to restrict the claimant's ability to work might be investigated.
- **Example:** An insurance company investigates a disability claim for a back injury after receiving a tip that the claimant has been seen participating in strenuous physical activities.
- **Property Damage Claims:** Claims for theft or property damage with suspicious details, such as pre-existing damage or inconsistencies in the timeline of events, might be investigated.
- **Example:** An insurance company investigates a jewelry theft claim after discovering the policyholder had recently inquired about increasing their jewelry coverage.

Gathering the Pieces: Methods Used in Insurance Investigations

Insurance investigators employ various strategies to assess the legitimacy of a claim:

- **Interviews:** Investigators interview the claimant, witnesses, and other relevant parties to gather information about the incident and verify details.
- **Surveillance:** Covert surveillance might be used to observe the claimant's activities and see if their actions contradict their reported limitations or injuries.
- **Evidence Collection:** Investigators meticulously collect and analyze physical evidence from the scene of an accident, stolen property, or damaged items to corroborate or refute the claimant's story.
- **Data Analysis:** Investigators may analyze medical records, employment history, and even social media activity to identify inconsistencies or discrepancies in the claim.

Balance and Ethics:

Insurance investigations must be conducted ethically and within legal boundaries. Investigators respect the privacy of claimants while diligently pursuing the truth. Open communication with policyholders and clear explanations about investigative procedures are crucial for maintaining trust in the system.

Protecting the System:

By uncovering fraudulent claims, insurance investigations ensure the sustainability of the insurance system. This, in turn, benefits honest policyholders by keeping premiums fair and ensuring resources are available for those who genuinely need them.

CHAPTER TWENTY-ONE

The Unsung Heroes: Legal Support Services in Action

The legal system can be complex and demanding. Attorneys rely on a network of legal support services to streamline processes, gather crucial information, and ultimately strengthen their cases. Let's explore the purpose of legal support services, the tasks they handle, and how they contribute to successful legal outcomes.

Shouldering the Load: The Purpose of Legal Support Services

Legal support services provide a vital support system for attorneys. Their primary goal is to:

- **Free Up Attorneys' Time:** By handling administrative tasks and time-consuming research, legal support professionals allow attorneys to focus on core legal strategies and client interaction.
- **Increase Efficiency:** Streamlined processes for tasks like document preparation and witness interviews ensure a smoother workflow and faster case resolution.

- **Enhance Case Strength:** Skilled legal support staff can uncover essential evidence, locate crucial witnesses, and conduct thorough research, ultimately strengthening the attorney's case.

From Research to Witness Stands: Use Cases for Legal Support Services

Legal support services encompass a wide range of tasks that contribute to a successful case:

- **Legal Research:** Legal support professionals conduct in-depth research on relevant laws, precedents, and legal arguments, providing attorneys with a strong foundation for their case strategy.
- **Example:** A legal support specialist researches a recent Supreme Court ruling on a specific type of employment discrimination claim. This research helps the attorney build a stronger case for their client.
- **Witness Location and Interviews:** Locating potential witnesses, conducting interviews, and preparing them for court appearances are crucial aspects managed by legal support staff.
- **Example:** A legal support professional identifies and interviews a neighbor who witnessed a car accident. Their detailed statement and potential court testimony can provide vital evidence for the client's case.
- **Evidence Gathering and Management:** Legal support services include collecting, organizing, and presenting evidence. This may involve requesting medical records, obtaining police reports, or preparing visual aids for courtroom presentations.
- **Example:** A legal support specialist retrieves a client's medical records to document the extent of their injuries

in a personal injury case.

- **Document Preparation and Management:** Legal support staff plays a key role in drafting legal documents, such as motions, briefs, and trial exhibits, ensuring accuracy and adherence to legal formatting requirements.
- **Example:** A legal support professional prepares a witness list and ensures all necessary legal documents are filed with the court within the stipulated deadlines.
- **Courtroom Assistance:** Legal support staff can provide valuable assistance during courtroom proceedings by managing exhibits, anticipating the attorney's needs, and ensuring a smooth flow of information.

Methods and Expertise:

Legal support professionals utilize a variety of skills and methods to execute their tasks effectively:

- **Research Skills:** The ability to research legal databases, case law, and relevant statutes is crucial for providing accurate legal information to attorneys.
- **Communication Skills:** Strong communication skills are essential for conducting witness interviews, drafting legal documents, and interacting with court personnel.
- **Organizational Skills:** Managing timelines, prioritizing tasks, and maintaining detailed records are essential for keeping cases organized and on track.
- **Technology Expertise:** Legal support professionals often utilize legal research software, case management systems, and other technology tools to streamline their work.

A Crucial Partnership:

Legal support services are the backbone of many successful legal practices. By taking on administrative tasks, conducting thorough research, and providing a strong support system, legal support professionals free up attorneys' time to focus on strategy and client advocacy. This collaborative approach ensures efficient case management and ultimately contributes to a stronger legal system for all.

CHAPTER TWENTY-TWO

Finding the Lost: Unveiling the Strategies of Missing Persons Investigations

The disappearance of a loved one can be a harrowing experience. Missing persons investigations aim to reunite missing individuals with their families, bringing closure and resolving a period of immense anxiety. Let's delve into the purpose of these investigations, the various reasons people go missing, and the methods employed to locate them.

Reuniting Families: The Purpose of Missing Persons Investigations

Missing person investigations serve two primary goals:

- **Locating the Missing Individual:** Utilizing various investigative techniques, investigators aim to find the missing person and ensure their safety.
- **Determining the Circumstances of the Disappearance:** Understanding the reason behind the

disappearance, whether it's accidental, voluntary, or due to foul play, can provide valuable information and guide the investigation.

A Multitude of Reasons: Use Cases for Missing Persons Investigations

People go missing for various reasons, prompting investigations to take different approaches:

- **Runaways:** Teenagers running away from home due to family conflict, emotional distress, or peer pressure require investigations that focus on their social circles and frequented locations.
- **Example:** An investigator might interview the runaway's friends, examine social media activity, and check for bus tickets or travel purchases to determine their potential destination.
- **Abductions:** When foul play is suspected, missing persons investigations work closely with law enforcement to analyze evidence, identify potential suspects, and track down leads.
- **Example:** Investigators might review CCTV footage from the area of the abduction, analyze witness statements, and collaborate with law enforcement to create a profile of the potential abductor.
- **Family Reunions:** In some cases, missing persons investigations help locate individuals who have lost touch with their families due to estrangement, memory loss, or other circumstances.
- **Example:** An investigator might use public record searches, social media platforms, and genealogical databases to track down potential relatives of the missing person.

Finding the Pieces: Methods Used in Missing Persons Investigations

Missing persons investigators employ a multi-pronged approach to locate missing individuals:

- **Database Searches:** Investigators utilize national missing person databases, DMV records, and social media platforms to search for any leads or sightings of the missing person.
- **Interviews:** In-depth interviews with family, friends, acquaintances, and anyone who might have seen the missing person before their disappearance are crucial for gathering information.
- **Collaboration with Law Enforcement:** Missing persons' investigations often involve close collaboration with law enforcement agencies, especially when foul play is suspected. Sharing information, analyzing evidence, and coordinating search efforts are essential for success.
- **Public Awareness Campaigns:** Distributing flyers, issuing press releases, and utilizing social media to spread information about the missing person can generate valuable leads from the public.

Time is of the Essence:

The initial hours and days following a disappearance are critical. Early reporting to law enforcement and initiating a missing person investigation can significantly increase the chances of a successful outcome.

A Beacon of Hope:

Missing persons investigations offer a lifeline to families during a time of immense emotional strain. By utilizing various investigative techniques, collaborating with authorities, and never giving up hope, these investigations can bring missing individuals home and provide families with the answers they desperately seek.

CHAPTER TWENTY-THREE

Following the Money Trail: Unveiling the Truth with Financial Investigations

Financial investigations delve into the world of money matters, aiming to uncover irregularities, hidden assets, or discrepancies in financial records. These investigations play a crucial role in various legal and business scenarios. Let's explore their purpose, the situations that necessitate them, and the methods investigators employ to follow the money trail.

Shining a Light on Finances: The Purpose of Financial Investigations

Financial investigations serve several key purposes:

- **Uncovering Hidden Assets:** In situations like divorce proceedings or probate cases, where a fair division of assets is crucial, financial investigations can identify hidden accounts, investments, or property that might not be disclosed initially.

- **Detecting Fraudulent Activity:** Businesses may utilize financial investigations to identify embezzlement schemes, money laundering operations, or other forms of financial misconduct.
- **Resolving Business Disputes:** Financial investigations can help resolve disputes between business partners by providing a clear picture of financial contributions, expenses, and potential discrepancies.

When Money Matters Most: Use Cases for Financial Investigations

Financial investigations are employed in various situations where a thorough examination of financial activities is essential:

- **Divorce Proceedings:** To ensure a fair and equitable division of assets during a divorce, financial investigations may be conducted to identify all marital assets, including hidden bank accounts, real estate holdings, or investments.
- **Example:** A forensic accountant might analyze a spouse's business expenses to identify potential attempts to conceal income or divert marital assets.
- **Probate Cases:** When settling the estate of a deceased individual, financial investigations can ensure all assets are accounted for and beneficiaries receive their rightful inheritance.
- **Example:** An investigator might examine the deceased's financial records to identify any outstanding debts or potential discrepancies in investment holdings.
- **Business Disputes:** In cases of shareholder disagreements or allegations of financial mismanagement, financial investigations can provide a

clear picture of a company's financial health and identify any potential wrongdoing.

- **Example:** A financial investigation might be conducted to verify the legitimacy of expense reports submitted by a company executive, following accusations of misuse of company funds.

Following the Paper Trail: Methods Used in Financial Investigations

Financial investigators utilize a variety of techniques to uncover hidden truths:

- **Tracing Funds:** Investigators use specialized tools and expertise to track the movement of money through bank accounts, wire transfers, and other financial transactions.
- **Financial Record Analysis:** Forensic accountants meticulously examine financial records, including tax returns, bank statements, and investment portfolios, to identify inconsistencies or suspicious activities.
- **Background Checks:** Conducting background checks on individuals involved in the case can reveal past financial irregularities or hidden business interests.
- **Data Analysis:** Financial investigators leverage data analytics tools to identify patterns in financial transactions that might indicate potential fraud or asset concealment.
- **Interviews:** Skilled investigators conduct interviews with key individuals, such as accountants, bankers, and business associates, to gather information and verify details.

Confidentiality and Legal Considerations:

Financial investigations must adhere to strict confidentiality regulations to protect sensitive financial information. Only authorized personnel should have access to the information gathered during an investigation. Furthermore, financial investigators must ensure their methods comply with all relevant laws and regulations.

Bringing Clarity to Complexities:

Financial investigations play a vital role in ensuring financial transparency and resolving complex legal and business disputes. By following the money trail, uncovering hidden truths, and providing a clear picture of financial activities, these investigations contribute to fair settlements, deter fraud, and ultimately promote financial integrity.

CHAPTER TWENTY-FOUR

Navigating the Digital Wild West: Unveiling Cyber Crimes with Cyber Investigations

The digital age has brought about a new frontier for crime – cyberspace. Cyber investigations combat these online threats and criminal activities, aiming to identify perpetrators, gather evidence, and protect individuals and organizations. Let's delve into the purpose of cyber investigations, the types of crimes they address, and the methods investigators use to navigate the digital landscape.

Guardians of the Digital Realm: The Purpose of Cyber Investigations

Cyber investigations serve several critical functions:

- **Identifying Cybercriminals:** By analyzing digital footprints and online activities, investigators aim to identify the individuals or groups responsible for cyberattacks, hacking attempts, or online fraud.

- **Gathering Digital Evidence:** Preserving and analyzing electronic evidence, such as log files, deleted data, and online communications, is crucial for building a strong case against cybercriminals.
- **Mitigating Cyber Threats:** Cyber investigations not only address past incidents but also help identify vulnerabilities in systems and networks, allowing organizations to implement stronger security measures and prevent future attacks.

When the Web Turns Dark: Use Cases for Cyber Investigations

Cyber investigations are employed across a spectrum of online criminal activities:

- **Hacking:** When a computer system is breached or sensitive data is stolen, cyber investigations identify the hackers, understand their motives, and retrieve stolen information.
- **Example:** Investigators might analyze network traffic logs, identify suspicious login attempts, and trace the hacker's IP address to pinpoint their location and apprehend them.
- **Online Fraud:** Cyber investigations play a vital role in uncovering online scams, phishing attempts, and identity theft schemes. The goal is to identify the perpetrators, recover stolen funds, and prevent future victims.
- **Example:** Investigators might analyze fraudulent websites, track online money transfers, and collaborate with financial institutions to freeze stolen funds.
- **Cyberbullying:** In severe cases of online harassment and cyberbullying, cyber investigations can identify the

perpetrators, preserve evidence of the abuse, and hold them accountable.

- **Example:** Investigators might analyze social media posts, trace online threats back to their source, and work with law enforcement to pursue legal action against the cyberbully.

Following the Digital Trail: Methods Used in Cyber Investigations

Cyber investigators utilize a specialized toolkit to navigate the complexities of the digital world:

- **Digital Forensics:** This involves recovering deleted data, examining electronic devices, and analyzing log files to reconstruct the sequence of events and identify the culprit's digital footprint.
- **IP Tracking:** Tracing the Internet Protocol (IP) address associated with a cyberattack or online activity can provide valuable clues about the perpetrator's location and internet service provider.
- **Analyzing Online Behavior:** Examining online activity patterns, social media posts, and communication history can help investigators identify the motives and methods used by cybercriminals.
- **Open-Source Intelligence (OSINT):** Gathering information from publicly available online sources, such as forums, social media, and data breaches, can provide valuable leads in cyber investigations.

Collaboration is Key:

Cybercrime often transcends geographical boundaries. Effective cyber investigations often require collaboration between law enforcement agencies, cybersecurity experts, and international partners to track down perpetrators and dismantle cybercriminal networks.

Protecting the Digital Frontier:

Cyber investigations play a crucial role in safeguarding individuals, businesses, and critical infrastructure from the ever-evolving threats of cybercrime. By employing cutting-edge technology and fostering collaboration, cyber investigators strive to create a safer and more secure digital environment for all.

CHAPTER TWENTY-FIVE

Crime Scene: A meticulous dance to secure the truth

Crime scene processing is a meticulous dance, a coordinated effort to gather the whispers of a crime and translate them into a clear voice for the investigation. It all starts with securing the scene – a perimeter is established to restrict access and prevent any potential contamination. This initial assessment is crucial, allowing investigators to grasp the bigger picture – the layout of the scene, the location of the victim (if any), and any immediate threats or hazards.

Once the scene is secured, investigators embark on a detailed documentation process. Using high-resolution cameras, they capture the scene from various angles, preserving the initial state of the evidence. These photographs become a visual record, a reference point for investigators throughout the case. In tandem with photography, meticulous sketches are created, diagramming the scene layout, the position of the victim or objects of interest, and the relationship between various pieces of evidence.

Now comes the heart of the process – evidence collection. Investigators meticulously sift through the scene, searching for any physical traces left behind by the perpetrator or the crime itself. Biological evidence like blood, hair, or fibers can be crucial for identifying suspects or placing them at the scene. Trace evidence, seemingly insignificant elements like soil or glass fragments, can hold hidden stories, revealing the movement of the perpetrator or the origin of a struggle. Firearm evidence, bullet casings and projectiles, can link the crime scene to a specific weapon. Documents and personal items, like IDs or letters, can offer insights into the victim or the circumstances of the crime.

Every step of evidence collection adheres to strict protocols to ensure its integrity. Investigators don sterile gloves and utilize specialized tools like tweezers to minimize contamination. Each piece of evidence is meticulously documented, photographed, and placed in an appropriate container to preserve its condition. This meticulous attention to detail ensures that the evidence speaks volumes in court, providing an unbiased account of the events that transpired. By following these steps, crime scene processing transforms a chaotic scene into a roadmap to the truth, paving the way for a successful investigation and ultimately, justice.

CHAPTER TWENTY-SIX

The Paper Trail: Documenting the Undisclosed Story

In the sterile silence of a crime scene, meticulous documentation becomes the voice of the voiceless. Investigators transform the chaos into a narrative, not with flowery prose, but with detailed, factual notes. These notes capture the essence of the scene – the weather conditions, the lighting, the overall layout of the room. They describe the location of the victim (if any), the positioning of furniture, and any unusual disturbances to the environment. A seemingly mundane detail, like a broken window on a cool night, could hold the key to reconstructing the timeline of events.

But documentation goes beyond the static scene. It chronicles the dynamic dance of evidence collection. As investigators sift through the area, their observations are meticulously recorded. The discovery of a bloody fingerprint on a shattered vase, a single hair caught on a window ledge – each detail is documented with precision. These notes not only serve as a memory jogger for investigators but also become a crucial reference point for presenting evidence in court.

The meticulousness extends beyond written records. Photographs, with timestamps and detailed captions, become a visual record of the scene, capturing details the human eye might miss. Sketches, drawn to scale and meticulously labeled, provide a spatial understanding of the scene, illustrating the relationships between various pieces of evidence.

Documentation doesn't end with the initial processing. The chain of custody, a chronological record of every individual who handled a piece of evidence, becomes paramount. Detailed logs trace the movement of evidence from the crime scene to the laboratory and back, ensuring its integrity is never compromised. A single break in the chain of custody can raise doubts about the evidence's legitimacy, potentially derailing a case.

Through detailed notes, comprehensive photographs, and an unwavering commitment to chain of custody, documentation becomes the silent partner in every investigation. It ensures that the whispers of the crime scene are not lost in the shuffle, but instead, are translated into a clear and compelling narrative for the courtroom.

CHAPTER TWENTY-SEVEN

Unveiling the Silent Witnesses: Processing Specific Evidence Types at Crime Scenes

Crime scenes are treasure troves of hidden stories, waiting to be unraveled. Each piece of evidence, no matter how seemingly insignificant, holds the potential to shed light on the events that transpired. Here's a glimpse into how investigators meticulously process specific evidence types to extract these silent whispers:

- **Bloodstains:** These crimson stains can be a wealth of information. Investigators meticulously document the location, size, shape, and pattern of bloodstains. This documentation can reveal the position of the victim or perpetrator during the crime, the direction of movement, and even the type of weapon used. After documenting, investigators collect samples using sterile swabs or cotton gauze. These samples are then packaged and transported to a laboratory for further analysis, potentially revealing the victim's blood type or even DNA profile.

- **Example:** At a crime scene, investigators discover a large, smeared bloodstain on the floor next to a broken vase. The pattern suggests a struggle, with the victim likely falling to the ground. Blood samples are collected from the stain and surrounding area for further analysis.
- **Fingerprints:** These unique identifiers can be a goldmine for investigators. Surfaces are meticulously dusted with fingerprint powder, a fine substance that adheres to the oils present in fingerprints. Once visible, the prints are carefully lifted using clear adhesive tape. The tape is then affixed to a fingerprint card for documentation and later analysis by fingerprint experts in the lab. These experts can compare the lifted prints to databases of known criminals, potentially identifying the perpetrator.
- **Example:** Investigators dust a doorknob near the crime scene entrance and discover a clear fingerprint. The lifted print is carefully packaged and sent to the lab for comparison against fingerprint databases. A match with a known criminal database entry could be a significant breakthrough in the investigation.
- **DNA:** Deoxyribonucleic acid, the blueprint of life, can be a powerful tool for identification. Investigators swab surfaces that might contain biological material, such as skin cells, hair follicles, or bodily fluids. These swabs are then packaged and transported to a forensic laboratory where DNA analysis can be conducted. A DNA profile obtained from the crime scene can be compared to known offender databases or potentially used to link a suspect to the scene.

- **Example:** Investigators swab a cigarette butt found near the crime scene. DNA analysis performed on the cigarette butt sample reveals a match with a known suspect, significantly strengthening the case against them.
- **Firearms:** These weapons require careful handling to prevent accidental discharge and preserve any potential fingerprints. Investigators wear protective gear and follow strict protocols when collecting firearms. The weapon is secured in a specialized container and transported to a laboratory for further examination. Ballistics experts can analyze the firearm to determine its caliber, match it to shell casings found at the scene, and potentially even link it to previous crimes.
- **Example:** Investigators locate a handgun near the victim's body. The weapon is carefully secured and transported to the lab for ballistics analysis. Matching the gun to shell casings found at the scene confirms it was the weapon used in the crime. Further analysis reveals the gun was used in a previous robbery, potentially connecting the two crimes.
- **Footwear Impressions:** These footprints left behind at the scene can be valuable clues. Investigators might employ different techniques depending on the surface. On soft surfaces like soil, a three-dimensional cast is made using a special molding material. On hard surfaces, high-resolution photographs are taken from multiple angles with a scale for reference. These impressions are then analyzed by footwear examiners who can identify the specific shoe brand, size, and even unique wear patterns, potentially linking a suspect to the crime scene.

- **Example:** Investigators discover muddy footprints near the crime scene exit. A cast is made of the footprints, which upon analysis by a footwear examiner, are identified as a specific brand of running shoe in a particular size. Security footage from a nearby store reveals a suspect wearing shoes matching this description, leading investigators to a potential lead.

By meticulously processing these various types of evidence, investigators transform a crime scene from a chaotic snapshot into a detailed narrative. Each piece, analyzed and interpreted, whispers its story, inching closer to the truth.

CHAPTER TWENTY-EIGHT

Securing the Secrets: Packaging and Labeling Evidence for a Flawless Investigation

Once the whispers of the crime scene have been meticulously collected through processing, the crucial task of packaging and labeling takes center stage. This seemingly mundane step plays a vital role in ensuring the integrity of evidence and the success of the investigation. Let's delve into the methods investigators employ to safeguard these silent witnesses:

Safeguarding the Story:

Contamination is the enemy of evidence. Investigators take every precaution to prevent any external elements from compromising the integrity of collected items. Paper bags become the preferred choice for breathable evidence like clothing or bloody fabrics. These bags allow the evidence to air out, preventing the growth of mold or mildew. For sturdier items or those with sharp edges, cardboard boxes or metal containers offer additional protection. Biological evidence like blood samples or swabs often finds its home in sealed plastic containers to prevent leakage or contamination from other materials.

The Importance of the Label:

Every piece of evidence, no matter how seemingly insignificant, deserves a voice. This voice comes in the form of a detailed label. The label acts as a passport for the evidence, documenting its journey throughout the investigation. Investigators meticulously record essential information on the label, including:

- **Case Details:** A clear reference to the case number ensures the evidence is always linked to the specific investigation.
- **Location:** Pinpointing the exact location where the evidence was found is crucial for understanding the context and potentially reconstructing the crime scene. For example, "Bloodstain found on living room carpet near the broken window" provides a detailed picture.
- **Date:** Recording the date of collection establishes a clear timeline and helps to prevent any questions about the chain of custody.
- **Collector's Initials:** Documenting who collected the evidence provides a clear audit trail and ensures accountability.

Examples:

- A bloody fingerprint lifted from a doorknob near the crime scene entrance would be placed on a labeled fingerprint card. The label would include the case number, "Doorknob, Main Entrance," the date of collection, and the investigator's initials.

- A bullet casing found near the victim's body would be placed in a sealed container labeled with the case number, "Bullet Casing, Found near Victim," the date of collection, and the investigator's initials.

By following these strict packaging and labeling protocols, investigators ensure that the evidence speaks for itself. The carefully secured packages and detailed labels become a silent testament to the meticulous care taken during collection, preserving the integrity of the evidence and strengthening the foundation for a successful investigation.

CHAPTER TWENTY-NINE

The Final Journey: Transporting Evidence to Unlock the Secrets

The meticulous dance of crime scene processing nears its conclusion. The evidence, carefully packaged and labeled, now embarks on its final journey to the forensic laboratory. Here, a team of skilled analysts will unlock the secrets held within each piece, transforming whispers into concrete information that can move the investigation forward.

Safe Passage:

The mode of transport depends on the nature of the evidence. For time-sensitive biological samples, refrigerated containers or even air courier services might be used to ensure they reach the lab in optimal condition. For more stable evidence like clothing or weapons, secure transport by police vehicle or certified courier services is employed. Throughout the transport process, proper documentation and chain of custody protocols are maintained.

The Importance of Storage:

Once at the lab, the evidence finds a temporary home in a secure, climate-controlled environment. This storage ensures the integrity of the evidence is maintained until it can be analyzed. For example, blood samples might be stored in a refrigerator, while digital evidence like computer hard drives might be kept in a Faraday cage to prevent any data corruption.

The Bigger Picture:

Meticulous crime scene processing is the cornerstone of a successful investigation. By carefully collecting, packaging, and transporting evidence, investigators ensure that the whispers of the crime scene reach the right ears – the skilled analysts in the forensic lab. These analysts, armed with advanced technology and expertise, can then unlock the secrets held within each piece of evidence. A bloodstain might reveal the victim's blood type or even the suspect's DNA profile. A fingerprint might identify the perpetrator. Gunshot residue on clothing could link a suspect to the crime scene.

Each piece of analyzed evidence becomes a brushstroke, painting a clearer picture of the events that transpired. This detailed picture strengthens the foundation of the investigation, allowing law enforcement to pursue the right leads and ultimately bring those responsible to justice. In conclusion, meticulous crime scene processing is not merely a technical procedure; it's a crucial step towards achieving truth and ensuring a fair outcome for all parties involved.

The Legal and Ethical Landscape

- Chapter 30: Walking the Tightrope: Legal and Ethical Considerations in Indian Investigations
- Chapter 31: The Moral Compass: Ethical Behavior in Indian Private Investigations
- Chapter 32: Navigating the New Legal Landscape: Opportunities and Challenges of the Bhartiya Nyaya Sanhita (BNS) and Bhartiya Sakshya Sanhita (BSS)
- Chapter 33: The Shifting Landscape: Opportunities and Challenges After the National DNA Profiling System (NDPS) and National Ballistics Information System (NBIS)
- Chapter 34: Legal Framework for Corporate Liability (This chapter likely fits better under Part 3: The Investigative Process)
- Chapter 35: The Labyrinth of Enforcement: Navigating Multi-Agency Investigations in India (This chapter could be placed under Part 3 alongside other investigative procedures)
- Chapter 36: Navigating the Evolving Landscape: Legal Considerations for Private Investigators in India
- Chapter 37: Navigating the Privacy Maze: Legal Boundaries for Private Investigators in India
- Chapter 38: The Ethical Imperative: Why Legal Compliance Matters for Private Investigators in India
- Chapter 39: Beyond the Law: Ethical Considerations for Private Investigators in India
- Chapter 40: The Delicate Dance: Balancing Privacy and Public Interest in Indian Private Investigations

CHAPTER THIRTY

Walking the Tightrope: Legal and Ethical Considerations in Indian Investigations

The world of private investigations in India demands navigating a delicate balance – adhering to the law while upholding ethical standards. Here's a breakdown of the key considerations:

1. **Respecting the Law:** Indian law sets boundaries for private investigators. They cannot engage in activities like impersonating law enforcement, tapping phones, or trespassing on private property. Understanding and following relevant laws is crucial to ensure the investigation is conducted legally and the evidence collected is admissible in court, if necessary.
2. **Confidentiality is Key:** A client trusts a private investigator with sensitive information. Maintaining confidentiality is paramount. This means keeping client details, investigation findings, and any collected

evidence strictly confidential.

3. **Integrity Above All:** Honesty and unbiased conduct are the cornerstones of ethical investigations. The investigator should avoid any personal biases or conflicts of interest. They should present the evidence objectively, highlighting both supporting and contradicting details.
4. **Professional Demeanor:** Maintaining professionalism throughout the investigation is vital. This involves treating everyone involved – clients, witnesses, and even potential suspects – with respect and courtesy.
5. **Avoiding Entrapment:** Investigators cannot create situations to induce someone to commit a crime. Their role is to gather evidence, not to manufacture it.

Building Trust and Maintaining Legitimacy: By adhering to these legal and ethical considerations, private investigators build trust with their clients and ensure the legitimacy of their investigations. Operating within legal boundaries protects them from legal repercussions, while upholding ethical standards fosters a sense of fairness and strengthens the credibility of their findings.

CHAPTER THIRTY-ONE

The Moral Compass: Ethical Behavior in Indian Private Investigations

The world of private investigations demands not just skill but also unwavering ethical conduct. Here's how investigators in India navigate the complexities of ethical decision-making:

- **Integrity Above All:** Honesty and transparency are the cornerstones of ethical investigations. Investigators avoid personal biases or conflicts of interest. They present the evidence objectively, highlighting both supporting and contradicting details.
- **Example:** An investigator discovers information during a background check that might cast doubt on the client's character. Despite the potential to upset the client, the investigator has an ethical obligation to disclose this information accurately and objectively.

- **Respecting the Law:** The boundaries of private investigation are clearly defined by law. Investigators cannot impersonate law enforcement, tap phones, or trespass on private property. They operate within legal parameters to ensure the evidence they gather is admissible in court, if necessary.
- **Example:** An investigator is tempted to plant a listening device in a suspect's office to gather incriminating evidence. However, knowing this is illegal and unethical, they resist this urge and focus on legal methods of surveillance, such as following the suspect in public places.
- **Confidentiality is Key:** A client trusts a private investigator with sensitive information. Maintaining confidentiality is paramount. This means keeping client details, investigation findings, and any collected evidence strictly confidential. Investigators cannot share this information with anyone unauthorized.
- **Example:** An investigator is approached by a friend who is curious about the details of a current case. The investigator politely declines, explaining their ethical obligation to maintain client confidentiality.
- **Avoiding Entrapment:** The investigator's role is to uncover the truth, not to manufacture it. They cannot create situations to induce someone to commit a crime. Ethical investigators rely on gathering evidence of existing wrongdoing, not creating opportunities for it.
- **Example:** An investigator suspects an employee of stealing from a company. They cannot approach the employee and offer them an opportunity to steal money as a way to catch them in the act. Instead, they would focus on finding evidence of past thefts, such as analyzing financial records or witness accounts.

The Investigator's Moral Code: Ethical behavior is not just a principle; it's the foundation of trust in private investigations. By upholding integrity, honesty, and respect for the law, investigators build strong relationships with clients and ensure their work contributes to achieving justice. They act as guardians of ethical conduct within the profession, setting a high standard for others to follow.

CHAPTER THIRTY-TWO

Navigating the New Legal Landscape: Opportunities and Challenges of the Bhartiya Nyaya Sanhita (BNS) and Bhartiya Sakshya Sanhita (BSS)

The enactment of the Bhartiya Nyaya Sanhita (BNS) and Bhartiya Sakshya Sanhita (BSS) marks a significant transformation in India's criminal justice system. These new codes, replacing the Indian Penal Code (IPC) and Indian Evidence Act (IEA) respectively, aim to modernize and streamline the investigative and judicial processes.

Let's delve into the potential opportunities and challenges that lie ahead:

Opportunities:

- **Enhanced Efficiency:** The BNS and BSS aim to simplify legal procedures, reducing delays and improving overall efficiency. This includes:
    - **Streamlined Investigation Processes:** The BNS introduces new provisions for search and seizure, arrest, and interrogation, potentially leading to more efficient and effective investigations.
    - **Clearer Admissibility of Evidence:** The BSS clarifies the rules for admitting and evaluating evidence, potentially reducing legal disputes and expediting trials.
- **Example:** Under the BNS, police officers are required to obtain a warrant before conducting a search, except in specific circumstances. This can prevent unlawful searches and seizures and ensure that evidence is obtained legally. The BSS, on the other hand, clarifies that electronic records, including emails and social media posts, are admissible as evidence, which can be crucial in prosecuting cybercrimes.
- **Stronger Protection for Victims:** Both codes emphasize victim rights and protection. This includes:
    - **Increased Victim Participation:** The BNS and BSS provide greater opportunities for victims to participate in the legal process, ensuring their voices are heard and their concerns are addressed.

  - **Enhanced Witness Protection:** Both codes introduce measures to protect witnesses, especially those considered vulnerable, encouraging them to come forward and provide crucial information.

- **Example:** The BNS mandates the establishment of Victim Support Units to provide assistance and guidance to victims throughout the legal process. The BSS also includes provisions for witness protection programs, including safe houses and anonymity measures.
- **Addressing Contemporary Crimes:** The BNS recognizes new categories of offenses, better reflecting the evolving nature of crime. This includes:

  - **Cybercrime:** The BNS introduces specific offenses related to cybercrime, such as hacking, identity theft, and online fraud, providing a legal framework to address these emerging threats.
  - **Organized Crime:** The BNS acknowledges organized crime as a distinct offense, allowing for more effective investigation and prosecution of criminal syndicates.

- **Example:** The BNS criminalizes the creation and dissemination of fake news, a growing concern in the digital age. It also introduces stricter penalties for organized crime offenses, deterring such activities and protecting society from their harmful effects.

Challenges:

- **Implementation and Awareness:** Effective implementation of the BNS and BSS requires extensive training for legal professionals, judges, and investigators. Raising awareness among the public about the new laws is also crucial.

- **Balancing Rights and Responsibilities:** The codes strive to balance the rights of accused individuals with the need for effective investigation and prosecution. This balance needs to be carefully maintained to ensure a fair and just legal system.
- **Adapting to New Offenses:** Law enforcement and judicial bodies need to adapt their approaches to investigate and prosecute new categories of offenses, such as cybercrime and organized crime. This requires specialized training and resources.
- **Inter-state Coordination:** The BNS and BSS are national laws, but their implementation and interpretation may vary across states. Effective coordination and consistent application are essential for uniform justice throughout the country.

The Path Forward:

The BNS and BSS represent a significant step towards modernizing India's criminal justice system. By addressing the challenges of implementation, awareness, balancing rights, adapting to new offenses, and ensuring inter-state coordination, these new codes have the potential to enhance efficiency, protect victims, address contemporary crimes, and ultimately deliver a more just and equitable legal system for all.

CHAPTER THIRTY-THREE

The Shifting Landscape: Opportunities and Challenges After the National DNA Profiling System (NDPS) and National Ballistics Information System (NBIS)

The implementation of the National DNA Profiling System (NDPS) and the National Ballistics Information System (NBIS) in India signifies a significant step towards a more robust investigative infrastructure. Here's a breakdown of the potential opportunities and challenges that lie ahead:

Opportunities:

- **Strengthened Forensics:** The NDPS creates a centralized database of DNA profiles, which can be a game-changer in criminal investigations. Investigators can use DNA evidence to:
    - **Link suspects to crime scenes:** DNA recovered from a crime scene can be compared to profiles in the NDPS, potentially leading to the identification of a suspect.
    - **Exonerate the innocent:** DNA testing can conclusively prove a person's innocence, especially in cases of mistaken identity.
    - **Investigate cold cases:** DNA evidence from unsolved cases can be re-examined and compared to profiles in the NDPS, potentially leading to new leads and bringing closure to families.

- **Example:** A serial sexual assault case has left the investigators frustrated. The NBIS helps identify a ballistic match between recovered shell casings from different crime scenes. This connects the cases and allows investigators to focus their efforts on a single suspect. DNA evidence from the crime scenes is then uploaded into the NDPS, potentially leading to a match with a known criminal or helping to exonerate a person wrongly accused based on circumstantial evidence.
- **Improved Ballistics Analysis:** The NBIS provides a centralized repository of ballistic information, including details about firearms used in crimes. This can benefit investigations in several ways:

  - **Tracing firearms:** Investigators can track the history of a firearm used in a crime, potentially leading them to the source of the weapon or identifying its previous owners.
  - **Identifying serial crimes:** The NBIS can help identify ballistic linkages between different crime scenes, indicating the possibility of a serial offender and allowing investigators to pool resources and share information.
  - **Firearms identification:** Recovered bullets or shell casings can be compared to the database, potentially identifying the specific firearm used in the crime.

- **Example:** A string of armed robberies across different states has left the police baffled. The NBIS helps investigators identify a match between the ballistics evidence from each crime scene. This confirms that the same firearm was used in all the robberies, indicating a possible organized crime ring. Investigators from different states can then collaborate, share resources, and apprehend the culprits.

Challenges:

- **Database Population:** The effectiveness of both NDPS and NBIS hinges on the comprehensiveness of their databases. Ensuring proper collection, storage, and analysis of DNA samples and ballistic information is crucial.
- **Privacy Concerns:** The creation of large-scale DNA databases raises privacy concerns. Strict protocols and regulations are needed to ensure the data's security and prevent misuse.

- **Infrastructure and Training:** Extracting maximum benefit from these systems requires robust infrastructure and well-trained personnel. Law enforcement agencies need to invest in training programs to equip investigators with the skills to utilize the NDPS and NBIS effectively.
- **Inter-state Collaboration:** For the NBIS to reach its full potential, seamless information sharing and collaboration between state police forces is essential. Standardized protocols and efficient communication channels need to be established.

The Road Ahead:

The NDPS and NBIS represent a significant step forward for forensic investigations in India. By addressing the challenges of database population, privacy concerns, infrastructure development, and inter-agency collaboration, these systems have the potential to revolutionize criminal investigations, leading to a higher rate of successful prosecutions, exoneration of the innocent, and ultimately a more efficient and just legal system.

CHAPTER THIRTY-FOUR

The Labyrinth of Enforcement: Navigating Multi-Agency Investigations in India

India's fight against white-collar crime is a complex dance, with multiple agencies vying to enforce the law. This multi-agency approach, while showcasing a strong commitment to accountability, presents its own set of challenges, making investigations intricate and demanding inter-agency cooperation amidst potential competition. Let's delve into this complex landscape with some illustrative examples:

A Multitude of Watchdogs:

- **Central Bureau of Investigation (CBI):** This premier agency investigates major financial crimes and corruption involving high-level officials.

- **Serious Fraud Investigation Office (SFIO):** The SFIO focuses on investigating companies for serious financial frauds like accounting manipulation or insider trading.
- **Enforcement Directorate (ED):** The ED tackles economic offenses like money laundering and foreign exchange violations.
- **Securities and Exchange Board of India (SEBI):** SEBI regulates the securities market and investigates market manipulation and insider trading by listed companies.

The Intertwined Dance of Cooperation and Competition:

Investigations into white-collar crimes often transcend the boundaries of a single agency's mandate. Here's where the complexities arise:

- **Inter-Agency Cooperation:** Effective investigations often require collaboration between agencies. For instance, the CBI might need to share information with the SFIO if a corruption case involves potential financial fraud by the accused official.
- **Example:** A government official is suspected of accepting bribes from a construction company in exchange for awarding contracts. The CBI investigates the bribery allegations, while the SFIO might simultaneously probe the construction company's financial records to uncover any evidence of money laundering or bid rigging. Success hinges on these agencies sharing information and coordinating their efforts.
- **Competition and Turf Battles:** Sometimes, competition between agencies can arise, with each vying for jurisdiction or credit for a high-profile case. This can

lead to delays in investigations or duplication of efforts.

- **Example:** A listed company's stock price plummets after allegations of accounting irregularities. Both SEBI and the SFIO might see this as falling under their purview, leading to a jurisdictional tussle that could delay the investigation.

Navigating the Labyrinth:

To overcome these complexities, several strategies are being employed:

- **Memorandums of Understanding (MoUs):** Formal agreements between agencies outline protocols for information sharing, joint investigations, and conflict resolution.
- **Joint Task Forces:** For complex cases, dedicated teams with personnel from multiple agencies can be formed to ensure coordinated action.
- **Centralized Monitoring:** A central authority might be established to oversee investigations and ensure cooperation between agencies.

The Road Ahead:

India's multi-agency approach to white-collar crime enforcement, while comprehensive, requires constant refinement. Fostering a culture of cooperation, streamlining information sharing protocols, and establishing clear jurisdictional boundaries are all crucial steps in ensuring a more efficient and effective fight against financial misconduct.

CHAPTER THIRTY-FIVE

Navigating the Evolving Landscape: Legal Considerations for Private Investigators in India

The world of private investigation in India is undergoing a period of transformation with the introduction of the Bhartiya Nyaya Sanhita (BNS). While there's still no specific law governing private detective agencies, understanding the BNS and existing legal principles is crucial for aspiring investigators.

A New Legal Framework: The BNS and its Implications

The BNS, replacing the Indian Penal Code (IPC), brings a new legal landscape that private investigators need to be aware of:

- **Privacy Rights under BNS:** The BNS potentially strengthens individual privacy rights. Investigators should be well-versed in relevant sections of the BNS that govern data protection, surveillance, and collection of personal information. Obtaining informed consent and respecting data privacy boundaries will be paramount.
- **Offenses under BNS:** The BNS outlines various offenses. Investigators should be familiar with sections related to trespass (potentially under Section 124 of BNS on Unlawful Entry), harassment (potentially under Section 198 of BNS on Stalking), and impersonation (potentially under Section 184 of BNS on Cheating by Personation). Understanding these provisions will help them avoid exceeding legal boundaries.
- **Respecting Law Enforcement Authority:** The BNS likely maintains the distinction between private investigation and law enforcement activities. Investigators should not engage in activities like arrests or searches without a warrant – powers reserved for law enforcement.

Building Trust: Ethical Practices Remain Key

Despite the evolving legal landscape, ethical conduct remains the cornerstone of a successful private investigation career in India:

- **Confidentiality:** Maintaining client confidentiality remains a core principle.
- **Transparency:** Being upfront about the methods used and the limitations of the investigation fosters trust with clients.

- **Accuracy:** Investigative findings must be accurate and unbiased. Maintaining meticulous records and employing reliable methods are crucial.

The Road Ahead: Adaptation and Advocacy

The BNS signifies a shift in the legal landscape, and private investigators will need to adapt their practices to comply with its provisions. Additionally, they can play a vital role in advocating for a more formal regulatory framework for the profession. Such a framework could establish licensing procedures, ethical codes, and clear boundaries between private investigators and law enforcement.

By staying informed about legal developments like the BNS, adhering to ethical principles, and advocating for a more formalized system, aspiring private investigators in India can navigate this evolving landscape and contribute to a professional and ethical investigative environment.

CHAPTER THIRTY-SIX

Navigating the Privacy Maze: Legal Boundaries for Private Investigators in India

The world of private investigation thrives on information, but venturing into the realm of personal data requires a deep understanding of privacy laws and boundaries. In India, the right to privacy finds strong backing in the Constitution and is further bolstered by the Information Technology Act 2000. Understanding these legal frameworks, especially with the recent introduction of the Bhartiya Nyaya Sanhita (BNS), is crucial for private investigators to operate ethically and avoid legal pitfalls.

The Constitutional Guarantee:

The Indian Constitution, under Article 21, guarantees the right to privacy. This fundamental right forms the bedrock of individual privacy protections in India. Private investigators must ensure their activities don't violate this right by:

- **Obtaining Informed Consent:** Before collecting any personal information about an individual, investigators must obtain their informed consent. This consent should be clear, specific, and voluntary, outlining the purpose of data collection and how it will be used.
- **Respecting Data Boundaries:** Investigators cannot collect personal information beyond what's necessary for the specific investigation they're conducting. Irrelevant data collection is a violation of privacy.

The BNS and Data Protection:

The BNS, replacing previous legislation like the Indian Penal Code (IPC), might introduce new provisions related to data protection. Investigators should stay updated on these developments and ensure their practices comply with any specific regulations regarding data collection, storage, and usage.

The Information Technology Act 2000: Guarding Electronic Data

The Information Technology Act (IT Act) 2000 plays a critical role in safeguarding electronic data privacy. Here's how it impacts private investigators:

- **Prohibition on Unauthorized Access:** The IT Act prohibits unauthorized access to computer systems or electronic data. Investigators cannot employ methods like hacking or malware to access personal information.
- **Surveillance Boundaries:** The Act restricts electronic surveillance. Investigators should avoid illegal wiretapping or other forms of electronic eavesdropping without a proper warrant.

Maintaining Ethical Boundaries:

Beyond legal restrictions, ethical considerations also play a vital role:

- **Transparency:** Clients have a right to know the methods investigators will employ. Being upfront about data collection practices fosters trust and avoids misunderstandings.
- **Data Security:** Investigators have a responsibility to ensure the security of any personal information they collect. Strong data security practices prevent unauthorized access or breaches.

The Road Ahead: A Balance Between Investigation and Privacy

The world of private investigation requires navigating a delicate balance between uncovering information and respecting individual privacy. By staying informed about legal developments like the BNS and the IT Act, obtaining informed consent, and adhering to ethical principles, private investigators in India can ensure their work is both effective and respectful of fundamental privacy rights.

CHAPTER THIRTY-SEVEN

The Ethical Imperative: Why Legal Compliance Matters for Private Investigators

In the world of private investigation, where shadows hold secrets and whispers turn into leads, adhering to legal boundaries isn't just a formality – it's the foundation for a successful and ethical career. Operating within the legal framework ensures the integrity of investigations, fosters trust with clients and authorities, and ultimately safeguards the credibility of the profession itself.

Maintaining Integrity: The Bedrock of Trust

Private investigators deal with sensitive information and often operate in a world of ambiguity. Clients entrust them with uncovering the truth, and legal compliance forms the bedrock of this trust. By adhering to laws like the Bhartiya Nyaya Sanhita (BNS) and the Information Technology Act 2000, investigators demonstrate their commitment to ethical practices and the legal boundaries that govern their profession. This builds trust with clients, who can be confident that their investigations are conducted with integrity and respect for the law.

Building Bridges with Law Enforcement

Private investigators are not vigilantes. They often collaborate with law enforcement agencies in their pursuit of the truth. Operating within the legal framework creates a bridge between these two entities. Law enforcement can trust that evidence obtained by investigators has been gathered legally and ethically, fostering cooperation and information sharing. This collaborative approach ultimately strengthens the pursuit of justice.

Public Confidence: The Cornerstone of Growth

The private investigation industry thrives on public trust. When investigators operate within legal boundaries, they project a professional image that inspires confidence in the public eye. This, in turn, can lead to increased business opportunities and a more robust private investigation sector. Furthermore, legal compliance helps to dispel negative stereotypes associated with the profession, replacing them with an image of ethical and responsible investigators.

The Peril of Illegality: A Lose-Lose Situation

Straying from the legal path can have severe consequences for both investigators and their clients. Evidence obtained illegally cannot be used in court, rendering the entire investigation a waste of time and resources. Clients could face legal repercussions if they knowingly use illegally obtained evidence. For investigators, the consequences can be even more damaging. They could face criminal charges, lose their licenses, and suffer irreparable damage to their reputation.

The Road Ahead: A Commitment to Ethical Practice

The path of legal compliance might seem arduous at times, but it's the only path that leads to sustainable success in the world of private investigation. By staying informed about legal developments, adhering to ethical principles, and prioritizing legal compliance, private investigators in India can build a strong foundation for their careers and contribute to a more professional and ethical investigative landscape.

CHAPTER THIRTY-EIGHT

Legal Framework for Corporate Liability:

It's important to clarify that as of today, July 13, 2024, the Bhartiya Nyaya Sanhita (BNS) and Bhartiya Sakshya Sanhita (BSS) are not yet implemented legislation in India. These bills were introduced in 2 tačiau (2023) but haven't been finalized or enacted.

However, we can discuss the existing legal framework for corporate liability in India and explore what potential changes the BNS and BSS might bring based on available information.

Current Landscape: A Mosaic of Statutes

Corporate criminal liability in India currently falls under the purview of various statutes, each with its own focus and penalties. Here are some key examples:

Impact of BNS and BSS on Corporate Liability Framework

The introduction of the BNS and BSS brings significant changes to the legal landscape for corporate criminal liability in India. Let's delve into these changes and how they might impact investigations:

- **Streamlined Framework:** The BNS, replacing the Indian Penal Code (IPC) and other criminal law statutes, potentially offers a more **unified and streamlined** approach to corporate criminal offenses. This consolidation could simplify the process of investigation and prosecution.
- **Enhanced Focus on Individual Accountability:** The BNS might introduce stricter provisions for attributing criminal liability to **individuals** within corporations. This could lead to a greater emphasis on holding directors, managers, and other responsible employees accountable for their actions.
- **Evidentiary Provisions in BSS:** The BSS, replacing the Indian Evidence Act, might introduce new provisions for gathering and handling **electronic evidence** in corporate crime investigations. This could be crucial in today's digital age, where much corporate activity takes place online.

Examples of Potential Changes:

- **Example 1:** A company's management team is found to have authorized a cyberattack on a competitor's IT systems. Under the BNS, the company and individual managers involved could be charged with a specific offense related to cybercrime, potentially leading to harsher penalties. The BSS might also provide clearer guidelines for collecting and analyzing digital evidence obtained during the investigation.
- **Example 2:** A manufacturing company is discovered to have been polluting a local river for years. The BNS might hold the company and its environmental compliance officers criminally liable for environmental

damage. The BSS could offer specific protocols for handling environmental samples and expert witness testimonies in such a case.

Uncertainties and Ongoing Developments

It's important to note that the BNS and BSS are recent enactments, and their full impact on corporate investigations will likely become clearer through court rulings and practical application. Further regulations and clarifications might also be issued to guide investigators and legal professionals.

By streamlining the legal framework, focusing on individual accountability, and potentially enhancing the handling of electronic evidence, the BNS and BSS aim to create a more robust system for holding corporations and their officials accountable for criminal activities. However, the true effectiveness of these changes will depend on their implementation and interpretation in the Indian legal system.

CHAPTER THIRTY-NINE

Beyond the Law: Ethical Considerations for Private Investigators in India

The world of private investigation is a complex dance between legality and ethical conduct. While adhering to the Bhartiya Nyaya Sanhita (BNS) and other legal frameworks is paramount, ethical considerations add another layer of responsibility for investigators in India. Here, we delve into some key ethical principles that guide a private investigator's actions:

Confidentiality: A Sacred Trust

Client information is the lifeblood of an investigation. Investigators have a fundamental ethical obligation to maintain complete confidentiality. This means:

- **Secure Storage:** Client data should be stored securely, using encryption and access controls to prevent unauthorized access.

- **Limited Disclosure:** Information should only be disclosed to authorized individuals directly related to the investigation and with the client's consent.
- **Avoiding Conflicts of Interest:** Investigators should avoid situations where their personal interests could conflict with their client's interests.

Transparency: Building Trust Through Openness

Building trust with clients is essential. Ethical investigators strive for transparency in their dealings:

- **Clear Communication:** Clients deserve to understand the scope of the investigation, the methods employed, and the potential limitations.
- **Managing Expectations:** Setting realistic expectations about timelines, costs, and potential outcomes is crucial for maintaining client trust.
- **Honesty in Reporting:** Investigators have a duty to present their findings honestly and objectively, even if the results are not what the client desires.

Respecting Boundaries: Moral and Legal Limits

The pursuit of truth shouldn't come at the cost of ethical or legal boundaries. Here's where ethical considerations come into play:

- **Avoiding Harassment:** Investigators should not engage in activities that harass or intimidate individuals during investigations.
- **Respecting Privacy:** Data collection and surveillance activities should be limited to what's necessary and conducted within legal and ethical bounds.

- **Truthfulness in interactions:** Investigators must avoid misrepresenting themselves or their purpose during an investigation.

Maintaining Professionalism:

Upholding a high standard of professionalism is vital for building a strong reputation:

- **Competence:** Investigators have a responsibility to continuously hone their skills and stay updated on legal developments and investigative techniques.
- **Objectivity:** Personal biases or prejudices should not influence the conduct of an investigation or the interpretation of findings.
- **Accountability:** Investigators should be accountable for their actions and be prepared to defend their methods and conclusions.

The Road Ahead: Building a Reputable Profession

Ethical considerations are the cornerstone of a thriving private investigation industry in India. By adhering to these principles, investigators can build a strong reputation for themselves and contribute to a more ethical and professional investigative environment. Ultimately, a commitment to ethical conduct not only benefits clients but also strengthens public trust in the profession as a whole.

CHAPTER FORTY

The Delicate Dance: Balancing Privacy and Public Interest in Private Investigations

The world of private investigations thrives on discretion and uncovering the truth. But in India, investigators operate within a complex dance – balancing the need for information with the fundamental right to privacy. Here's why ethical considerations and professional conduct are paramount:

- **Respecting Privacy Rights:** The Indian Constitution guarantees the right to privacy. Private investigators must tread carefully, ensuring their methods don't violate this right. Imagine a skilled investigator navigating a maze, knowing they can't breach certain walls to gather information. Legal methods like background checks through authorized channels or public record searches become essential tools.

- **Public Interest vs. Individual Privacy:** Sometimes, investigations involve a potential conflict – public interest might seem to outweigh individual privacy. For instance, a private investigator might be hired to uncover corruption within a company. While gathering evidence, they might stumble upon personal information not directly related to the case. A strong ethical code ensures the investigator prioritizes the legitimate purpose of the investigation while safeguarding irrelevant personal information.
- **Maintaining Client Trust:** Clients entrust investigators with sensitive information. Upholding ethical principles builds trust and demonstrates the investigator's commitment to protecting confidential client data. Imagine a locked vault – the investigator safeguards the client's secrets within this vault, ensuring no unauthorized access.
- **Avoiding Legal Trouble:** Operating ethically protects investigators from legal repercussions. Illegal surveillance, unauthorized data collection, or privacy violations can lead to lawsuits and damage the investigator's reputation. Ethical conduct keeps the investigator on the right side of the law, avoiding a potential legal nightmare.

Complying with Established Laws: India has several laws governing privacy, including the Information Technology Act, 2000. Understanding and adhering to these laws is crucial for ethical investigators. These laws define what constitutes personal information, set limitations on data collection and storage, and outline specific procedures for lawful interception of electronic communication. By complying with these legal frameworks, investigators ensure their methods are not only ethical but also legally sound.

Conclusion: Ethical conduct is not just a suggestion for private investigators in India; it's a necessity. By respecting privacy rights, maintaining a delicate balance between public interest and individual rights, and operating within the boundaries of the law, investigators can build trust with clients, protect themselves from legal issues, and contribute to a more professional and ethical private investigation industry.

CHAPTER FORTY-ONE

Industry Standards and Guidelines: Safeguarding Professionalism and Ethical Conduct

In the realm of private investigations in India, adhering to industry standards and guidelines goes beyond simply avoiding legal trouble. It's about establishing a foundation for professionalism, ensuring the integrity of investigations, and ultimately, delivering unbiased, fair, and accurate results. Here's how these standards and guidelines contribute to a more ethical and trustworthy private investigation industry:

- **Maintaining Objectivity:** Industry standards often emphasize the importance of objectivity. Investigators should avoid preconceived notions or biases that could influence their findings. Imagine an investigator approaching a case like a balanced scale, meticulously weighing all evidence without tipping the scales towards a predetermined outcome.

- **Transparency with Clients:** Clear communication with clients is crucial. Investigators should be transparent about their methods, fees, and limitations. This builds trust and allows clients to make informed decisions throughout the investigation process. Think of the investigator as a guide, keeping the client informed on every step of the journey and openly discussing limitations or potential roadblocks.
- **Confidentiality and Data Security:** Client information and any sensitive data collected during an investigation must be kept confidential. Industry standards often prescribe data security protocols to safeguard this information. Imagine the investigator operating with a secure vault, ensuring only authorized personnel have access to confidential data, and implementing measures to prevent unauthorized breaches.
- **Respect for Individual Rights:** As discussed earlier, respecting individual privacy rights is paramount. Industry standards often reiterate legal limitations on data collection and surveillance methods. This ensures investigations are conducted within the bounds of the law and avoid infringing upon the rights of individuals not directly involved in the case.
- **Accuracy and Verification:** Investigative findings hold weight only if they are accurate and verifiable. Industry standards emphasize the importance of thorough research, meticulous record-keeping, and verification of information from multiple sources. Imagine the investigator as a meticulous fact-checker, double-checking every detail and ensuring the final report is

built upon a foundation of verifiable evidence.

- **Maintaining Professional Relationships:** Investigators often collaborate with law enforcement agencies, legal professionals, and other investigators. Industry standards promote maintaining respectful and professional relationships with these stakeholders. This fosters a collaborative environment where information can be shared effectively, leading to more comprehensive investigations and ultimately, a fairer justice system.

By adhering to established industry standards and guidelines, private investigators not only uphold ethical principles but also elevate the professionalism of the entire industry. This commitment to ethical conduct fosters trust with clients, strengthens the legal defensibility of investigative findings, and paves the way for a future where private investigations in India are synonymous with reliability, integrity, and the pursuit of truth.

CHAPTER FORTY-TWO

Transparency and Honesty: The Cornerstones of Trust in Private Investigations

In the world of private investigations, where shadows often hold the key to the truth, transparency and honesty become the investigator's guiding light. Building trust with clients and ensuring the integrity of investigations hinge on these fundamental ethical principles. Here's why transparency and honesty are cornerstones of the profession:

- **Client Trust: The Foundation of Success:** Clients entrust investigators with sensitive information and the pursuit of often-critical matters. Transparency fosters trust by keeping clients informed about the progress of the investigation, the methods employed, and any unexpected challenges that might arise. Imagine the investigator as an open book, readily sharing relevant information with the client and fostering a collaborative environment.

- **Avoiding Misconceptions and Misunderstandings:** Clear and honest communication from the outset is essential. Private investigators should avoid exaggerating their capabilities or making unrealistic promises about the outcome of an investigation. Setting realistic expectations from the beginning builds trust and prevents misunderstandings later. Think of the investigator as a roadmap provider, outlining the potential paths the investigation might take and the estimated timeframe for reaching the destination.
- **Respecting the Rights of All Individuals:** Honesty extends beyond communication with clients. Investigations must be conducted with respect for the rights of all individuals involved, not just the client. Investigators should avoid deceptive tactics or misleading individuals to gather information. Imagine the investigator approaching each person with respect, relying on legitimate methods to gather information, and never resorting to lies or manipulation.
- **Maintaining Legal and Ethical Boundaries:** Transparency goes hand-in-hand with ethical conduct. Investigators should be upfront with clients about the legal limitations of their work. Certain methods, like illegal surveillance or unauthorized data collection, are not only unethical but also carry legal repercussions. Honesty ensures the investigation stays on the right side of the law and avoids compromising the integrity of the findings.

- **Building a Positive Reputation:** In the competitive world of private investigations, a reputation for honesty and transparency is invaluable. By conducting themselves with integrity, investigators earn the trust of not just clients but also other professionals within the industry, fostering a more collaborative and ethical environment. Think of the investigator as building a strong brand, where honesty and transparency are the hallmarks of their service, attracting clients who value a fair and ethical approach.

Transparency and honesty are not merely ideals; they are essential practices that define a responsible and ethical private investigator. By prioritizing these principles, investigators can build strong client relationships, ensure the integrity of their work, and contribute to a more trustworthy and respected private investigation industry in India.

CHAPTER FORTY-THREE

Navigating the Legal Labyrinth: Ensuring Legal Compliance in Private Investigations

In the world of private investigations, where uncovering the truth often involves navigating hidden corners, legal compliance becomes the compass that guides ethical and successful investigations. Stepping outside the boundaries of the law can not only jeopardize the integrity of the investigation but also lead to serious legal consequences for the investigator. Here's why legal compliance is paramount:

- **Maintaining the Investigation's Integrity:** An investigation built on a foundation of illegal methods is like a house constructed on unstable ground. Evidence obtained through unlawful means, like illegal surveillance or unauthorized data collection, might be deemed inadmissible in court, rendering the entire investigation a waste of time and resources. Legal compliance ensures evidence is gathered through legitimate methods, safeguarding the integrity of the investigation and the defensibility of its findings.

- **Protecting Investigator Credibility:** Operating within the legal framework protects an investigator's credibility and reputation. Legal repercussions for breaking the law can damage an investigator's career and erode the trust of clients and other professionals within the industry. Compliance with legal guidelines ensures the investigator maintains a good standing and earns respect as a professional operating within the boundaries of the law.
- **Understanding the Legal Landscape:** The legal landscape governing private investigations in India can be complex. Understanding relevant laws, such as the Information Technology Act, 2000, and the Indian Penal Code (IPC), is crucial for investigators. Knowing what constitutes legal methods for data collection, surveillance, and information gathering empowers investigators to operate with confidence. Imagine the investigator as a skilled navigator, adept at reading legal maps and charting a course that stays within the designated boundaries.
- **Obtaining Necessary Permissions:** Certain investigative actions might require obtaining specific permissions. For instance, accessing phone records or conducting physical surveillance in certain situations might necessitate legal authorization. Understanding these requirements and diligently following them ensures the investigation operates within the legal framework. Think of the investigator as a responsible driver, obtaining the necessary permits (like a license) before embarking on their investigative journey.

- **Avoiding Legal Trouble:** The consequences of legal non-compliance can be severe. Investigators who break the law can face fines, imprisonment, or even professional sanctions. Following legal guidelines protects investigators from legal repercussions and allows them to focus on conducting their investigations with confidence.

Conclusion: Maintaining ethical standards goes hand-in-hand with legal compliance. By prioritizing both, private investigators can build trust with clients, stakeholders, and the public at large. This commitment to ethical and legal conduct ultimately strengthens the credibility of the private investigation industry and paves the way for a future where private investigators are valued partners in the pursuit of truth and justice, operating within the legal framework of India.

Glossary Of Important Terms For Private Investigators

This glossary provides definitions for key terms you'll encounter throughout your career as a private investigator in India.

- **Affidavit:** A written statement of fact confirmed by oath or affirmation, used as evidence in court.
- **Bail Enforcement:** The act of apprehending a person who has failed to appear in court after being released on bail (also known as bounty hunting).
- **Chain of Custody:** A documented record tracing the handling of evidence from its collection to its presentation in court, ensuring its authenticity.
- **Civil Case:** A legal case involving a dispute between private parties seeking compensation or enforcement of a right.
- **Client:** The individual or entity who hires a private investigator to conduct an investigation.
- **Confidentiality:** The obligation to keep information obtained during an investigation secret, except when legally required to disclose it.
- **Data Collection:** The process of gathering information electronically or otherwise, often for investigative purposes.
- **Embezzlement:** The fraudulent appropriation of property entrusted to one's care.
- **Ethics:** The moral principles that guide a profession and its members.
- **Evidence:** Any information presented in court to prove or disprove a claim.
- **Felony:** A serious crime punishable by imprisonment

for a year or more.

- **Information Technology Act, 2000:** A law governing information technology, electronic records, and offenses related to computers.
- **Indian Penal Code (IPC):** The main criminal code of India.
- **Industry Standards and Guidelines:** Established best practices and ethical principles that guide private investigators.
- **Investigation:** A systematic inquiry into a situation or event to gather facts and uncover the truth.
- **Jurisdiction:** The legal authority of a court to hear and decide a case.
- **Misdemeanor:** A less serious crime punishable by a fine or short-term imprisonment.
- **Objective:** Unbiased and neutral, avoiding personal opinions or prejudices.
- **PDAR Bill (Private Detective Agencies (Regulation) Bill):** A proposed legislation aimed at regulating the private investigation industry in India.
- **Plaint:** A formal written complaint filed with a court to initiate a civil case.
- **Privacy Laws:** Laws protecting the right to privacy from unlawful government intrusion or disclosure of personal information.
- **Public Interest:** A concern for the welfare of the community as a whole.
- **Surveillance:** The close observation of a person or place to gather information.
- **Transparency:** Openness, honesty, and clear communication.

This glossary is not exhaustive, and new terms may emerge as the legal and investigative landscapes evolve. It's recommended to stay updated on relevant legal developments and industry terminology.

List Of Relevant Resources For Private Investigators In India

- Websites:
- Ministry of Home Affairs, Government of India: https://www.mha.gov.in/en (Provides information on legal frameworks and law enforcement)
- Law Commission of India: https://lawcommissionofindia.nic.in/ (Offers resources on legal reforms and proposed legislation, including the PDAR Bill)
- Bar Council of India: https://www.barcouncilofindia.org/ (Provides information on the legal profession and ethical guidelines for lawyers)
- Association of Private Detectives and Investigators (APDI): https://www.apdi.in/ (Industry association offering membership, resources, and events for private investigators)
- The Indian Society for Private Detectives (ISPD): https://www.apdi.in/ (Industry association promoting professional standards and ethical conduct)
- Books:
- The Law of Private Investigators in India by Rajesh Chopra (A comprehensive guide to legal aspects of private investigations in India)
- The Indian Evidence Act by R.K. Jain (A detailed explanation of the law governing evidence admissibility in Indian courts)
- Ethical Investigations by Tom Curry (Explores ethical considerations and best practices for conducting

investigations)

- Surveillance for Beginners by David Brininstool (Provides an introduction to legal and ethical surveillance techniques)
- The Art of Investigation by Colin Wilcox (Offers practical guidance on conducting effective investigations)
- Professional Organizations:
- Association of Private Detectives and Investigators (APDI): (Membership organization offering training programs, networking opportunities, and professional development resources)
- The Indian Society for Private Detectives (ISPD): (Membership organization promoting ethical conduct, professional development, and collaboration within the industry)
- American Society for Industrial Security (ASIS): https://www.asisonline.org/ (International organization providing resources and professional development for security professionals, including private investigators)
- Additional Resources:
- Subscribe to legal publications and industry newsletters to stay updated on relevant developments.
- Attend workshops, conferences, and seminars offered by professional organizations or legal institutions.
- Consider pursuing certifications or continuing education courses to enhance your investigative skills and knowledge.
- Remember, this list is not exhaustive, and new resources may emerge. It's crucial to stay proactive in seeking knowledge and refining your skills throughout your career as a private investigator in

India.

Beyond The Case: Charting Your Course As An Ethical Indian Private Investigator

We hope this handbook empowers you to navigate the exciting and challenging world of private investigations in India. Remember, ethical conduct is not a destination; it's a continuous journey. By upholding these principles and staying up-to-date with the evolving legal landscape, you can ensure a successful and fulfilling career as a private investigator.

www.ingramcontent.com/pod-product-compliance
Lightning Source LLC
LaVergne TN
LVHW021155160826
845679LV00024B/2123

* 9 7 9 8 8 9 4 9 8 2 6 8 7 *